D1711278

Tribal Dispossession
and the
Ottawa Indian University Fraud

UNIVERSITY OF OKLAHOMA PRESS : NORMAN

Tribal Dispossession and the Ottawa Indian University Fraud

by William E. Unrau and H. Craig Miner

By William E. Unrau

The Kansa Indians: A History of the Wind People (Norman, 1971)
The Kaw People (Phoenix, 1975)
The End of Indian Kansas (with H. Craig Miner) (Lawrence, Kans., 1978)
Tending the Talking Wire (Salt Lake City, Utah, 1979)
The Emigrant Indians of Kansas (Bloomington, Ind., 1979)
Tribal Dispossession and the Ottawa Indian University Fraud (with H. Craig Miner) (Norman, 1985)

By H. Craig Miner

The St. Louis-San Francisco Transcontinental Railroad (Lawrence, Kans., 1971)
The Corporation and the Indian (Columbus, Mo., 1976)
The End of Indian Kansas (with William E. Unrau) (Lawrence, Kans., 1978)
Wichita: The Early Years (Lincoln, Nebr., 1982)
The Rebirth of the Missouri Pacific (College Station, Texas, 1983)
Tribal Dispossession and the Ottawa Indian University Fraud (with William E. Unrau) (Norman, 1985)

Library of Congress Cataloging in Publication Data

Unrau, William E., 1929-
    Tribal dispossession and the Ottawa Indian University fraud.

    Bibliography: p.
    Includes index.
    1. Ottawa Indians—Land transfers. 2. Ottawa University (Kan.)—History. 3. Ottawa Indians—History. 4. Indians of North America—Kansas—Land transfers. 5. Indians of North America—Kansas—History. I. Miner, H. Craig. II. Title.
E99.09U67 1985   978.1'00497   84-19534
ISBN 0-8061-1896-2 (alk. paper)

The paper in this book meets the guidelines for permanence and durability of the Committee on Production Guidelines for Book Longevity of the Council on Library Resources, Inc.

To Robert G. Athearn, our teacher and friend

Contents

Illustrations

Preface

IN THE COURSE of working through certain special inventories in the Civil and Natural Resources Division of the National Archives for the purpose of preparing a general study of Indian removal from Kansas, we retrieved a bulky file simply designated "Ottawa University." An examination of these documents led to the identification of others, including special files, briefs, transcripts of litigation, minutes, correspondence, and other manuscript material contributing to a picture of what had happened to the Ottawa Indians during their brief and disastrous residence in Kansas. We decided that this story, including earlier events in Ohio and the Great Lakes area and later in Oklahoma, deserved full narration. Indian removal was as complex as it was tragic, and it is our hope that the Ottawa experience will shed some additional light on this dark era of Indian-white relations.

Several persons made important suggestions and provided valuable assistance in obtaining the material necessary for this project. John Porter Bloom, Robert M. Kvasnicka, and Richard C. Crawford, of the National Archives, gave freely of their time and professional experience. Dr. Bloom's assistance at a particularly difficult stage in the research deserves special mention and thanks. Joseph Snell, Robert W. Richmond, and Eugene Decker, of the Kansas

State Historical Society; Reed Whitaker, of the Federal Records Center in Kansas City; Thoburn Taggert, Jr., Dale Schrag, and the late Russell Dybdahl, of the Wichita State University Library staff; James A. Clifton, of the University of Wisconsin-Green Bay; R. David Edmunds, of Texas Christian University; Ronald A. Averyt, of Ottawa University; Patrick A. Hayes, of the Bureau of Indian Affairs, Washington, D.C.; Michael Heaston, of Austin, Texas; and Fleming Gottlieb, of Cleveland, Ohio, cooperated to the fullest extent, as did officials of the Native American Rights Fund in Boulder, Colorado, and the Ottawa University Business Office in Ottawa, Kansas.

Finally, we wish to thank Jackie Cummins for clerical assistance and Dean Lloyd Benningfield and the Wichita State University Research Committee for financial support.

WILLIAM E. UNRAU
H. CRAIG MINER

Wichita, Kansas

Tribal Dispossession
and the
Ottawa Indian University Fraud

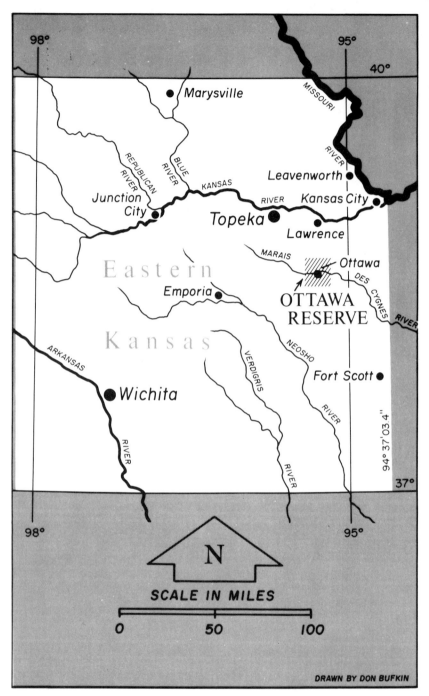

Eastern Kansas, including the Ottawa reservation and the town of Ottawa. Drawn by Don Bufkin and reproduced with permission from *Arizona and the West* 25, no. 3 (Autumn, 1983).

1

Searching for Lost Justice

FEW WOULD DENY that education, in the broadest sense, is a primary component of our national institutional structure. In his famous Farewell Address delivered nearly two hundred years ago, President George Washington declared: "Promote, then, as an object of primary importance, institutions for the general diffusion of knowledge. In proportion as the structure of government gives force to public opinion, it is essential that public opinion should be enlightened."[1] Jefferson, certainly no less a champion of intellectual improvement, committed much of his public and private career to the advancement of education and, especially, to the ideal of genius and virtue in the service of the republic. The argument that freedom and education were mutually dependent elements of the democratic dream was the very lifeblood of such legislation as the Land Ordinance of 1785, the Morrill Land-Grant Act of 1862, and in our century, the Economic Opportunity Act of 1964. As the midtwentieth-century *Report of the President's Commission on Higher Education* concluded, "It is commonplace of the democratic faith that education is indispensable to the maintenance and growth of freedom of thought, faith, enterprise, and association. . . . [It] is at once to insure equal liberty and equal opportunity to differing individuals and groups, and to enable the citizens to under-

stand, appraise, and redirect forces, men, and events as
these tend to strengthen or to weaken liberties."[2]

If measured in sheer numbers and locations, those who
planned and attempted to develop institutions of higher
learning in antebellum America were successful. One educational leader described the United States in 1851 as "a
land of colleges." Thirty years later the chief executive of
Columbia University was prompted to wonder how it was
that England, with its population of 23 million, could manage with only four degree-awarding institutions, while in
America the state of Ohio alone was somehow able to support no fewer than thirty-seven.[3] Many, of course, were
sponsored and operated by the aggressive and increasingly
fragmented Christian denominations. By the time Andrew
Jackson had taken residence in the White House, American Christendom, principally evangelical Protestantism,
had divided and subdivided to such a degree that the
leaders of nondenominational colleges felt gravely threatened and frustrated regarding the future of higher learning in general. In 1834 the president of the nondenominational University of Nashville explained:

> A principal cause of the excessive multiplication and dwarfish
> dimensions of Western colleges is, no doubt, the diversity of
> religious denominations among us. Almost every sect will have
> its college, and generally one at least in each state. . . . This
> is a grievous and growing evil. Why colleges should be sec-
> tarian, any more than penitentiaries or than bank, road or
> canal corporations, is not very obvious. . . . Must every State
> be divided and subdivided into as many college associations
> as there are religious sects within its limits? And thus, by
> their mutual jealousy and distrust, effectually prevent the
> usefulness and prosperity of any one institution?[4]

In fact, there were so many pre-Civil War colleges in
large measure because of the absence of any strong sentiment favoring state-controlled, or what some called a mo-
nopolistic, system of higher education. President James
Monroe's several attempts to establish a national univer-

sity in Washington, D.C., became mired in the sands of
the states-rights controversy and the chief executive's conviction that such action would require a constitutional
amendment. The increasing fluidity of class and social
distinctions in the developing West encouraged the belief
that a university education was not only a privilege but a
right of every adult American, with the result that the
allegedly decadent European tradition of institutions for
the select few gave way to a literal host of "colleges for
the people." In 1856 one egalitarian educator asserted:

> It is one of the glories of our American colleges, that their
> doors are alike open to all classes in society. . . . Within the
> walls of an American college all factitious distinctions vanish.
> There the rich and the poor not only meet together, but they
> commence their intellectual struggle under a full knowledge
> of the fact that no hereditary dignity or inherited wealth . . .
> can . . . repress the aspirations of genius.[5]

As proved to be the case in Ottawa, Kansas, the mania
for college building was closely identified with land speculation. Denominational aggrandizement, lofty theories of
class fluidity, and often exaggerated statements regarding
the genius of American education could not disguise the
fact that an extremely effective method of promoting in-
fant towns was to make the enterprise the seat of a college or university. Not a few institutions were known as
"real estate colleges"—purely and simply commercial ventures, like banks, turnpikes, canals, and various retail and
wholesale ventures. On the other hand, given the erratic
character of the American economy between 1815 and the
Civil War, it is hardly surprising that speculation in higher
education was a hazardous undertaking. Certainly the sta-
tistics bear this out. In the frontier states of Alabama,
Tennessee, Missouri, Mississippi, Texas, Arkansas, and
Kansas, for example, over 90 percent of the 246 colleges
founded before the Civil War failed. In Florida the failure
rate was 100 percent, while the more established state of
Virginia experienced a failure rate of 69 percent.[6]

One way to minimize the risk in sparsely settled regions, such as the future Kansas-Nebraska Territory, was to secure a government subsidy in the form of cheap, or even free, land. The often extensive realties of the American Indians presented such opportunities. Generally tribal lands were held under judicial authority, but increasingly they were jeopardized by the government's emerging "civilization" program. As a remnant group of the repeatedly displaced Ottawa people of the Great Lakes region eventually came to understand, promises of facilities for educational advancement could be manipulated, distorted, and even broken—especially in the remote and virgin prairies of eastern Kansas. There the Ottawas were promised a university; there they paid for most of it; and there—and in the offices of East Coast bureaucrats—they lost it. What follows is a case study of manipulation and fraud.

As those things went in the nineteenth century, it was a rather paltry steal—approximately $42,000 worth of Ottawa tribal funds remained unaccounted for. But thanks to several investigations at several levels of accountability —and the findings of the Indian Claims Commission in the twentieth century—the clandestine maneuvers and the misuse of Ottawa resources by enterprising white invaders were recorded in great detail.[7] Also, because the Ottawa Indian University fraud involved a complex confrontation between Indian traditionalists, Indian nontraditionalists, government officials, territorial and state bureaucrats, and white educational speculators, it demonstrates the structure of intercultural contact at that time, as well as how nineteenth-century entrepreneurs and Christian missionaries viewed themselves and their presumed world mission. What emerges is not at all a simple story, with heroes and villains clearly identified and conveniently arrayed on one side or the other for the consumption of true believers in white duplicity or outright native barbarism.

It is at best an oversimplification to argue that we already know how specific Indian groups were dealt with in this period, based on general studies of Indian dispossession in Kansas.[8] In fact, each individual case is unique, and to ignore them is to take an attitude profoundly ahistorical. The point of view of this study is micro- rather than macrocosmic. Surely it is more productive to understand the structure of an atom than to speculate glibly about the ultimate character of the universe.

Except for the Indian Claims Commission records and the files of the various attorneys who over the years have been involved in Ottawa litigation, the documents of this incident have gathered dust in the National Archives and elsewhere for well over a century. While some of the many fragments of the story were recognizable or familiar to the actual participants of that time, the very complexity of the Ottawa fraud provided a significant challenge to contemporary observers, as it does to historians committed to a generalized view of Indian-white conflict. We hope that we have made a modest step toward a general understanding of the case. We offer no apology either for taking a restrained moral stance or for passing judgment on certain legal, economic, or simply utilitarian actions. It seems particularly imperative to judge with candor, because it is a major conclusion of this study that legalism and pragmatism were the intellectual stalking-horses that contributed most to the victory of economic interest over human concern in Kansas's Ottawa country in the nineteenth century. That a defense must be offered for introducing the moral dimension, despite the important studies of Indian dispossession that share our approach,[9] only reinforces the rather frightening truth that the climate of opinion in ways directly relevant to this study has changed little during more than a century. One of the purposes of history is to demonstrate what alternatives existed in the past and may prevail in the future, thus allowing the informed (and concerned) citizen at least an opportunity to alter the status quo. This cannot be done without applying undeniable facts to basic judgments.

Moral timidity and eventual moral breakdown characterized the champions of tribal acculturation in nineteenth-century Indian Kansas. To explain the actions of Clinton Carter Hutchinson, the Ottawa Indian agent and town promoter, without branding him as an ethical chameleon, would require a profound distortion of rational investigation. For him the present was never fixed—the real world was a place where advantage was to be grasped by those willing to shift position as opportunities presented themselves, regardless of human consequences. And more frequently than not, those opportunities were created and energized by his own self-righteous behavior and his conception of "Providence." Similar performances can be observed in the behavior of the other principal characters in this drama: Enoch Hoag, the Quaker Indian superintendent; John Tecumseh (Tauy) Jones, the mixed-blood tribal leader; Robert Atkinson, the Baptist superintendent of the Ottawa University Board and educational troubleshooter; and the Reverend Isaac Kalloch, whose alleged sexual indiscretions in New England and elsewhere were moral pabulum compared with his later activities among the Ottawas in Kansas.

In addition, the Ottawa case encourages moral analysis because it was precisely in the name of education and morality that the fraud took place. The devices that were used in forwarding the establishment of Ottawa University were just those elements of culture most revered by the dominant white society at that time: education, religion (that is, Christianity), and the law. It may be argued that the involvement of the principal figures in the financial aspects of the operation—as opposed to their philosophical justifications of it and their use of economic and legal weapons in promoting the university—ensured that the Baptists' plan, which might have benefited the Ottawas, damaged and sullied both its white advocates and the Indians whom it was supposed to benefit. This practical involvement crippled the powers of analysis of the would-be educators, stunted their perceptions, and compromised their empathy with anyone outside their own circle. It was this very kind of obstruction and special-interest response that one century later led the Special Senate Subcommittee on Indian Education to conclude that the nation's policies and programs for educating American Indians were a profound national tragedy.[10]

In practice, substantive considerations became cloudy and often gave way to procedure, while failure to keep morality in the forefront encouraged the Ottawa educators to work in league with the federal bureaucracy of that time. Investigators of the Indian University succumbed to their own devices. The tribe was permanently split into "progressive" and "traditionalist" factions. Thus villains and victims changed places as the complex game uniting high purpose and self-interest lost its mooring in a sea of factionalism. What the nineteenth-century participants described as "good sense" or "expediency" or "progress" regarding the Ottawa Indian University may be more accurately characterized as moral fatigue.

Still in operation at its original location about fifty miles southwest of Kansas City, Ottawa University presently advertises itself as an innovative collegiate institution affiliated with the American Baptist Churches, U.S.A. It proudly proclaims itself to have been "[f]ounded by Baptists in 1865 on land given by the Ottawa Indians," and its administrators have recently announced a plan to provide tuition and boarding scholarships to members of the Ottawa Tribe of Indians certified by Ottawa Chief Lewis H. Barlow of Miami, Oklahoma (who also serves as an honorary member of the University Board of Trustees).[11] Presumably the program is an attempt to make some restitution for the past and, perhaps, to forestall further litigation under Article 6 of the Ottawa Treaty of 1862, which provided that a 20,000-acre parcel of tribal land was to be used for the purpose of endowing a school for the benefit of the Ottawas.[12] Lawsuits are no absolute solution now any more than in the past, and they can damage and benefit people blameless of any crime or virtue—people who often are uninformed regarding developments of the past. Repeated legal maneuvering encourages the instrumentalist greed in which the original injustice may have had its origin, just as histories do that shun central issues, even if they happen to be moral.

Where then is such justice as may be found at this late date to be discovered? Perhaps the answer is to achieve a level of understanding sufficient to discourage the repetition of such schemes. No broad and sweeping generalizations will illuminate the many complex and often cleverly conceived interrelationships that led to the failure of Ottawa University as an institution of learning for Indians. It is the objective of this study to isolate and attempt to understand the more important details of the deception practiced by the university's promoters, to hint at the nature of its many companions elsewhere in the West, to place the evidence in historical context, and to suggest rational alternatives at the more critical junctures in place and time.

A few words regarding the word "fraud" in the title of this study. The authors have relied on a combination of several definitions offered in *The Oxford English Dictionary:* (1) the quality or disposition of being deceitful; faithlessness; insincerity (now rare); (2) criminal deception; the use of false representations to obtain an unjust advantage or to injure the rights or interests of another; and (3) all deceitful practices in defrauding or endeavoring to defraud another of his known right, by means of some artful device, contrary to the plain rule of common honesty (mid-nineteenth-century legal definition).[13] Having examined a considerable body of letters, reports, petitions, and legal briefs, it is especially the phrase "plain rule of common honesty" that has most impressed the authors as having direct applicability to the case at hand. We have also been guided by Francis Jennings' admonition:

> Some persons may find it incredible that the righteous, god-fearing folk who were their ancestors could have engaged in such practices as are here described. . . . Persons and groups reaching for illicit power customarily assume attitudes of great

moral rectitude to divert attention from the abandonment of their own moral standards of behavior. Deception of the multitude becomes necessary to sustain power, and deception of others rapidly progresses to deception of self. All conquest aristocracies have followed such paths. It would be incredible if ours had not.[14]

2

The Ottawas and the Invader

THE THREE GROUPS of Ottawa Indians who signed the treaty in 1862 that provided the tribal funding for the first major Indian university west of the Mississippi River were known as the "Ottawas of Blanchard's Fork of the Great Auglaize River," the "Ottawas on the Little Auglaize River residing at Oquanoxie's village," and the "Ottawas residing near the places called Roche de Boeuf [Cattle Point] and Wolf Rapids, on the Miami [Maumee] River of Lake Erie." All of those locations were in northwestern Ohio, in the Maumee River valley southwest of present-day Toledo. The Blanchard's Fork group were located near present-day Ottawa, in Putnam County; Oquanoxie's village was near Oakwood, in eastern Paulding County; and the Roche de Boeuf group resided on the right bank of the Maumee near Waterville, in Wood County.[1]

By the Treaty of Detroit (1807) the Blanchard's Fork group had been officially recognized by the federal government, and by the Treaty at the Rapids on the Miami [Maumee] of Lake Erie (1817), Oquanoxie's people and the Roche de Boeuf group had received similar recognition. Those were neither the first nor the final deliberations between these Indians and the United States, nor was there any general agreement then or later as to whether those particular bands and their leaders were authoritative spokesmen for the Ottawa nation in general. Indeed, as late as the early 1950s, under Docket No. 133 of the United States Indian Claims Commission, the issue of traditional tribal organization, geographical location, and political leadership were once again examined.[2] That case, which eventually was consolidated with ten other ICC dockets of similar character,[3] traced broadly some of the more controversial aspects of Ottawa ethnography, from the first white contacts in the early seventeenth century to the recent past, without resolving the specific issues of tribal organization to the satisfaction of all petitioners.

Historically speaking, an important consequence of that litigation was to reaffirm the long-standing Anglo-American insistence that there exists a recognizable central authority (whether real or questionable) when dealing with Indian people in the diplomatic sense. When that negotiating technique fails, the next tactic is usually to identify diverse elements in a tribe, work through the various factions, encourage them to pull at cross purposes, and then deal with the emergent "leaders" most amenable to change —a strategy that worked well in the establishment of Ottawa Indian University.

Particularly significant to an understanding of the Ottawas' difficulties in nineteenth-century Kansas was the tribe's diversity dating back to before the initial white contacts. The most recent scholarly summary of the Ottawas—which incidentally fails to mention the university fraud—complains, "A partial explanation for the inadequate treatment [of] the Ottawas . . . may lie in the great number and diversity of sources on their culture and history, none of which, however, gives a full and coherent account."[4] In a similar vein, another recent, but more general, account simply states, "Very few historians have attempted to write about the Ottawa people in general terms."[5] Such statements place the university fraud in a critical, historical context.

A key point in understanding the uncertainty of early Ottawa history is the mobility of the tribe. No precise location has been established for an exclusive Ottawa village before the decade of the 1660s, nearly half a century after first European contacts. Samuel de Champlain had reported encountering a group of three hundred Ottawa men near the mouth of the French River above Georgian Bay in 1615. In the following year, perhaps in late January or early February, after spending time with the Petuns (or Tobacco Nation) west of Lake Ontario, the same French official visited a larger body of Ottawas at some point on Bruce peninsula. "[W]e left that place [of the Petuns]," wrote Champlain, "and went to a nation of savages which we named the Cheveux Relevés [the Ottawas], who were very much delighted to see us again. . . . This tribe is very large and most of its members are great warriors, hunters and fishers. They have several [chiefs], each of whom commands in his own region."[6]

Champlain's reference to the Ottawas as the "Cheveux Relevés" simply meant that he and his men were impressed by the Ottawa style of wearing their hair dressed high and carefully groomed. Most significant was his observation that they recognized various political leaders who seemed autonomous in their respective locations. Subsequent references confirm that diversity, both in names and descriptions of the tribal organization. The Jesuit Bressani's report of 1663, for example, referred to the Ottawas as the "Ondatauauat"; while in his report of 1664-65, Claude Allouez, S.J., called them the "Outaouax" or "Outaoucas." Still another variation was that of Jacques Marquette, who in 1669 termed them the "Outaouak."[7] Even as late as 1851, Henry R. Schoolcraft, who served as a government agent for the Ottawas at Sault Sainte Marie, used the name "Ottawa." Modern scholarship has suggested that the Ottawas were Algonquian speakers of a southeastern Ojibwa dialect and that the most typical rendition of their apellation was "Odawa" or "Adawe," meaning "to trade" or "to buy and sell."[8] Certainly their commerce in furs, skins, medicinal herbs, sunflower oil, cornmeal, and mats with the French and Indian peoples of the Great Lakes region was notable.

From Potawatomi accounts handed down orally over many generations, it is believed that the Ottawas, Chippewas, and Potawatomis were one nation that at a remote time penetrated the Great Lakes region from the northeast. Some seventeenth-century written sources do, in fact, use the term Ottawa as a general name for the great wave of Algonquians who journeyed to Montreal for purposes of trade. And in the nineteenth century it was not uncommon for agents of the United States government to designate one group as the "United Chippewas, Potawatomis, and Ottawas," particularly when negotiating land-cession treaties. To complicate matters further, individuals and small bands from one village would establish residence at another village, so that on occasion formal adoptions would take place and original identities would become blurred or completely forgotten. For example, John Tecumseh (Tauy) Jones, who was important in Ottawa tribal history, was born a half-blood Canadian Chippewa. He received some white education in New York and Kentucky and then went west to join the Potawatomis on their reservation immediately west of Missouri. Following disagreements over religion and his personal interest in a plot of tribal land, he abandoned the Potawatomis and took up residence with the Blanchard's Fork and Roche de Boeuf Ottawas in nearby Kansas. They in turn formally adopted him and granted him a variety of valuable personal concessions before finally expelling him. Thus with solid evidence Jones could, by the early 1860s, describe himself as a "Chippewa-Potawatomi-Ottawa."[9]

Chippewa legends are more specific regarding a separation between the three groups. According to these accounts, a division occurred at the Straits of Mackinac no later than the sixteenth century, after which the Chippewas traveled north and west, the Potawatomis migrated down the eastern shore of Lake Michigan, and the Ottawas remained at the Straits. Recent studies by linguists, however, point to an Ottawa and Chippewa separation from the Potawatomis at an earlier date, perhaps at a point somewhere above the Great Lakes. In addition, archaeological evidence suggests that Potawatomi social and settlement patterns in late prehistoric times were more similar to those of the Dumaw Creek "prairie" culture in west-central Michigan (c. 1600 A.D.) than those of the Ottawas and Chippewas.[10]

It can at least be said that possible precontact differences between these northern Algonquians were more a matter of degree than kind. This relativity extends even into the middle of the seventeenth century, when the Ottawas were more differentiated from the Chippewas and Potawatomis. Apart from the highly subjective tribal self-identifications, some seventeenth-century sources used the term Ottawa to refer not only exclusively to a local group called the Sable but also to the aggregate of Sable, Sinago, Nassauakueton, Kiskakon, and Michabou groups who, in concert with other Algonquians, constituted the entire wave of Indians who came down to Montreal to trade.

Even as late as 1851, in reporting the "Names of the Divisions of the Group" based on laws, treaties, or usage, Schoolcraft reported the existence of no less than fifteen different groups of Ottawas—fourteen located in "Indian Territory W." and the remaining in Michigan. Eight years later, on the basis of a personal visit to the Roche de Boeuf and Blanchard's Fork Ottawas' reservation in eastern Kansas Territory, Lewis Henry Morgan went so far as to state that the Ottawas had "lost their tribes [i.e., their gens, or clan, structure] except [as] they call themselves after places they have occupied." While Morgan's oversimplified observations were derived from his belief that all Indian groups had a common gens organization at the time of the Columbian invasion, and that failing to find this in a particular instance meant that the original structure had been "lost," his statement nevertheless foreshadowed the more recent view of ethnologist William V. Kinietz, who has testified that at no time did the Ottawas have a head chief over all the separate groups, nor did they ever have a continuous tribal council. Today a considerable number of the Ottawas simply state that all Ottawa people originated from one of three great families: the Michabou, or Great Hare; the Namepich, or Carp; and the more obscure Bearpaw.[11]

Before the removal of the Roche de Boeuf and Blanchard's Fork groups to a government-designated reservation west of Missouri in the mid-1830s, there were nearly four dozen Ottawa villages or territories surrounding the Great Lakes—principally in the Grand and Maumee river valleys, in the Traverse Bay area, and on the Manitoulin Islands farther north. In the Great Lakes region the Ottawas had a diverse economy based on a plentiful supply of natural resources. While the women collected maple sap, wove mats, and planted beans, corn and squash, the men engaged in hunting, fishing, and trapping. In time the latter activity became increasingly important. Following a vicious struggle in the 1640s between the Hurons and the Iroquois over access to French fur merchants, a substantial body of Ottawas in 1654 established themselves as the principal middlemen between the tribes of the Old Northwest and the French at Montreal, and for the next three decades they provided nearly two-thirds of France's New World fur supply.[12]

The steady westward movement of the French culminated in the establishment by La Mothe-Cadillac in 1701 of a settlement and a fortification on the Detroit River. That and overtrapping by the Ottawas and their tribal neighbors undermined the Ottawa fur monopoly. Private French traders, determined to challenge or even to ignore the four government monopolies awarded by Detroit commander Henry Tonty, went into business on their own. Knowing full well that a few monopolies were driving the prices of goods higher, the Indians joined ranks with the private traders to such a degree that Boishébert, Tonty's successor, was ultimately forced to sell trading permits to anyone who would apply.

As more and more traders converged on Detroit, particularly those whose credit in Montreal was shaky or wholly lacking, bickering ensued and intertribal warfare intensified. The situation was further aggravated by the colonial struggle then raging between the French and British, which led to a vicious Fox-Iroquois attack on Detroit near the close of Queen Anne's War (1702 to 1713). Strained relations between the Ottawas and the Miamis led to open conflict, as for example, in 1708 when a French-sponsored Miami party attacked the Ottawas near Detroit. Additional competition in the fur trade was presented by the Wyandots and the Shawnees on the south, who were being courted by British traders led by George Croghan of Pennsylvania. Even the Ottawas were prompted to modify their long-standing economic ties with the French in favor of the British.[13]

While the changing complexion of the international fur trade encouraged the Ottawas to settle at more strategic locations and form new associations in accord with their own economic interests, the introduction of alcohol and epidemic disease by the Europeans served as a catalyst for abrupt changes. Brandy, of course, was a major commodity in the fur trade; to the invaders it was as profitable as it was devastating to the Indians. Tightening of the French supply, as happened in 1730, required adjustments in the Ottawa economy, and it prompted them to look to the English south of the Great Lakes for a more dependable supply. An added attraction was the English capacity to provide a great variety of goods of higher quality than the French, often at cheaper prices.[14]

Those adjustments were in themselves not irreparably disorientating to Ottawa society—in fact, they encouraged the Ottawas' adaptive tendencies. More serious were the disruptions caused by the eruption of epidemic smallpox. In the absence of reliable and comprehensive population data, particularly before the founding of Detroit in the middle of the seventeenth century, it is difficult to discuss Ottawa demography with precision. Nevertheless, it is clear that smallpox figured heavily in the general depopulation of the Algonquian peoples that began with the first great epidemic in New England in 1616-17. During the years from 1633 to 1641 an almost uninterrupted series of small-pox epidemics broke out in the Great Lakes-Saint Lawrence River region. In 1681, for example, it was reported that the disease was so severe among the Ottawas that they were prevented from bringing their pelts to Montreal. This particular epidemic seems to have been introduced by private "vagabond" traders, against whom the French authorities were unwilling to lodge official complaints, possibly because they wanted to discredit these traders in the eyes of the suffering Indians. Erratic and large-scale movements both of Indians and of Europeans during the French and Indian War rekindled the fires of the dreaded disease, and near the close of the eighteenth century one major Ottawa village on upper Lake Michigan lost nearly 50 percent of its inhabitants. The survivors of that tragedy attributed the disease to the recent visit of a Catholic priest from Canada. Apart from the obvious despair and suffering brought on by these epidemics, an important consequence was the further scattering of villages and decentralization of the Ottawa political structure. Some protection came from vaccine provided by the United States government early in the nineteenth century, but by then other forces were even more powerful in the fragmentation of the various Ottawa groups.[15]

Throughout the era of French dominance in the fur trade of the Great Lakes, the Ottawas displayed considerable skill in playing the English against the French as a means of satisfying their dependency on the technology and cultural paraphernalia of Western Europe. Until Detroit fell to the British at the close of the French and Indian War (1760), the Ottawas were without rivals in the game of shifting allegiances, not only with the French and

British but also with neighboring tribes as well. In a strategy that one recent authority has termed "ascendancy," the Ottawas engaged in manipulative alliances with the Hurons, the Foxes, the Kickapoos, the Mascoutens, and the Miamis. On occasion they went so far as to abandon their close Potawatomi kinfolk, particularly when the latter proved too steadfast in their support of the French. The Ottawas' strategy was not even altered by the extended struggle between the Foxes and the French-sponsored Potawatomis, Sauks, Miamis, Kickapoos, Mascoutens, Weas, and Pianka-shaws, which culminated in the bloody massacre of nearly three hundred Fox men, women, and children in September, 1730. When confronted with the turbulence of Euro-pean colonial competition and Native American resistance, the Ottawas placed personal survival at the very center of their relations with others.[16]

The actions of the Roche de Boeuf and Blanchard's Fork Ottawas are examples of this strategy in practice. In the decade between the Fox massacre and the outbreak of the second major colonial war between France and Britain in 1740 (King George's War), the French were frustrated by the increasing power of the British traders in the Old Northwest. In response the French determined to lease their major western posts to the highest bidders, with the hope that the revenue from these leases would help balance the budget for their New World ventures. It was a serious mistake. To offset the cost of the leases, the French traders were forced to sell their goods to the Indians at a higher price. As more and more British traders moved into the Ohio country with cheaper goods, the French problems were further complicated by the British blockade of the Saint Lawrence during the early stages of King George's War. The duplicity of the powerful Hurons at Sandusky, the continued fear of smallpox outbreaks in and around the French posts, intertribal bickering at Detroit, and the practical consideration that with the advance of the British traders into the Ohio country it no longer was necessary to travel so far to dispose of pelts, all these factors caused the Ottawas to abandon the Detroit area and establish villages on the Maumee and its tributaries southwest of Lake Erie. By the 1750s there were major Ottawa settlements at Roche de Boeuf and Wolf Rapids on the Maumee, at Blanchard's Fork of the Great Auglaize, on the lower Little Auglaize, and on the Cuyahoga River to the east. A few of the more venturesome Ottawas journeyed farther south to the upper Wabash country and the English traders who awaited them there. Some of the scattered bands who remained behind joined with the Chippewas to destroy French property at Detroit and to murder several French traders as far north as Michilimackinac.[17]

Despite these important population shifts, a century of social and economic contact was not easily forgotten, and a substantial number of Ottawas remained loyal to the French during the early stages of the French and Indian War—the last great colonial war between France and Britain. Ottawas, principally from the Detroit area, provided Captain Pierre de Contrecoeur and Captain Daniel de Beaujeu support in the French defeat of the British General William Braddock at Fort Duquesne in 1754. They provided critical manpower in the struggle against the British at Niagara. They provided important garrison support at a number of French posts in the Great Lakes region, and they played a major role in the French defense of Detroit. Only when it became absolutely certain that the French cause in North America was futile did they indicate a willingness to come to terms with the British. With Louisburg, Niagara, Duquesne, and Quebec in the hands of the British in the closing months of 1759, the Ottawas followed the logic of necessity by casting their lot with the only remaining European power that could guarantee the kind of life to which they had become accustomed. Four years later the celebrated and much misunderstood event known variously as the Conspiracy of Pontiac, Pontiac's Uprising, or the Revolution of Pontiac was less the result of the famous Ottawa leader's desire to seek revenge against the British than it was the result of British administrative bungling, particularly by Lord Jeffrey Amherst, and gross failure to provide the regular supply of gifts and trade goods that the Ottawas fully expected after the expulsion of the French from North America. And Pontiac's ultimate failure to forge a powerful pan-Indian movement against the British in 1763 was less the product of British perseverence and diplomatic prowess than of general Indian factionalism.[18]

A similar opportunism and adjustment to the realities of armed conflict can be seen in the actions of the Ottawas during the later stages of the American Revolution. After characteristically vacillating in making a firm commitment to the British cause, the Maumee Ottawas were quick to announce their support of the Virginians after George Rogers Clark's spectacular occupation of the British post at Vincennes in February, 1779. To the frustrated British commandant, Jacques Lernoult, they simply announced, "We now tell you that we are going to our brothers the Virginians, with whom we will make & receive that which is good." While most of the Detroit Ottawas remained loyal to the British, their southern kinsmen joined a Spanish force from Saint Louis who in February, 1781, attacked the British at Fort Saint Joseph, near present-day Niles, Michigan, and seized a major store of goods from the traders resident there. Certainly at the end of the American Revolution there were few Ottawas who believed they had been defeated by anyone, nor were they convinced that their land titles had been relinquished to either the British or the Americans.[19]

But the Americans were flushed with the diplomatic victory in Paris that gave them control of the area between the Appalachians and the Mississippi River, and they saw matters otherwise. Less than two months after the signing of the Treaty of Paris on September 3, 1783, Congress under the recently ratified Articles of Confederation decreed that, because the Ottawas and other tribes of the Old Northwest had supported the British during the war, they had forfeited their claims to the Ohio country. In a gesture of friendship that was an obvious tactic to discourage further Indian cooperation with the British, the Americans allowed the Ohio tribes to continue to reside there on small reservations; but they would be expected to enter into separate treaty negotiations that would allow the clearing of land titles for American occupation of at least part of their domain. Encouraged by the British and plagued by disunity, a few of the Ottawas participated in the treaties of Fort McIntosh (1785) and Harmar (1789), which authorized land cessions and a boundary between Indian and non-Indian land in central Ohio. Yet those treaties were meaningless because they never were put into effect. Continued Indian resistance revealed that Indian unity against the invading Americans was still a possibility. The sorry spectacle of American General Josiah Harmar's military campaign up the Maumee River in the fall of 1791 was followed by Governor Arthur St. Clair's even worse defeat the following year by a combined Indian force at Fort Recovery on the upper Wabash.

Still anticipating support and supplies from the British, whose interest in the area seemed genuine, the Ottawas and their Indian allies refused to abandon their farms and villages without a fight. What they failed to understand was the British fear of an open confrontation with the Americans that might endanger their posts on the north. Nor were they able to gauge the bellicose attitude of white squatters and land jobbers, who believed that the federal government had a moral obligation to clear title to an area that for too long had been in the hands of unproductive natives. No less a person than Secretary of State Thomas Jefferson advised Charles Pinckney, in November, 1793, that negotiations with the northwest tribes had failed completely and that the only recourse was war. Congress finally provided the troops and military leadership that produced General Anthony Wayne's defeat, and the severe demoralization of the shaky Indian confederacy, at Fallen Timbers, in August, 1794, at the very doorstep of the Roche de Boeuf Ottawa settlement. The invasion of the Long

Knives (as the Indians called the invaders) had begun in earnest.[20]

The resultant Treaty of Greenville, concluded on August 3, 1795, and proclaimed the following December 2, was an historical watershed of momentous proportions. Even though the negotiations lasted for nearly two weeks, it was apparent to all that the Indians had no real bargaining power. They knew that they had been defeated and could no longer depend on the British for support. Southern Ohio had been lost, and the entire southern Great Lakes region on the north lay vulnerable to future white penetration. Joining the chiefs and headmen of eleven other tribes, including their Potawatomi and Chippewa relatives, Ottawa leaders Augooshaway, Keenoshameek, La Malice, Machiwetah, Thowonawa, and Sacaw agreed to a boundary between Indian and non-Indian land that began at modern-day Cleveland and ran up the Cuyahoga River to Fort Laurens, then west to Fort Recovery, and finally south to a point on the Ohio River just east of present-day Madison, Indiana.

It is true that the Roche de Boeuf and Blanchard's Fork settlements were spared for the time being, but since the treaty provided for more than a dozen federal reservations north of the Greenville Treaty line, as well as free passage by both land and water to the various military posts located on those reservations, the Maumee Ottawas had little reason to view the future with optimism. The nearly 50,000 acres of land that General Wayne had reported under Ottawa cultivation was the very kind of terrain the Long Knives coveted. While article 5 of the treaty did allow the Indians to hunt, plant, and dwell on their lands "so long as they please," this concession did not preclude the government's right of preemption. The same article included the guarantee that, "when those tribes, or any of them, shall be disposed to sell their lands, or any part of them, they are to be sold only to the United States."[21]

During the more than four decades between the Treaty of Greenville and the Miami (Maumee) River removal treaty of 1831, the dozens of Ottawa groups scattered in modern Michigan and Ohio were subjected to the relentless pressure of white advances and the continuing instability of Anglo-American relationships. Directly or indirectly, the often confusing stipulations of treaties negotiated at Detroit in 1807; Brownstown, Indiana, in 1808; Spring Wells, Michigan Territory, in 1815; Fort Meigs, Ohio, in 1817; Saint Marys, Ohio, in 1818, and Chicago in 1821 demonstrated that, compared to their northern brethren, the Ohio Ottawas were for the most part able to hold their own against the land-hungry whites who violated the Greenville line. Only when the government's ostensibly flexible plan of removal was stripped of its ethnocentric rationalizations, and the more subtle plan for tribal "civilization" had taken its toll, did the Roche de Boeuf and Blanchard's Fork Ottawas think seriously about relocating west of the Mississippi.[22]

The pressure of white advance was particularly severe in Ohio. Three days after the Greenville line had been formalized, a prominent land speculator wrote that a horde of settlers from Kentucky, Virginia, and Pennsylvania were "running mad" into the area west of the Great Miami. "They almost laugh me full in the face when I ask them one dollar per acre for first-rate land," said John Cleves Symmes, "and tell me they will soon have as good for sixty cents." That same year Northwest Territorial Governor Arthur St. Clair complained of confusion regarding the government's practical intentions and warned that if something were not done soon it would be extremely difficult to remove the squatters. By 1799 the territorial electorate had selected expansionist-minded William Henry Harrison as their first congressional delegate. Under his and Albert Gallatin's guidance the legislative branch passed a new land ordinance allowing for a much reduced minimum land purchase and a liberal credit system for the purchaser. Within the next two decades the states of Ohio, Indiana, and Illinois had been created, and by 1830 the white population of the Old Northwest had increased to nearly 1.5

million from an 1800 total of just over 50,000 persons. Not unexpectedly, the vast majority settled in the area south of a line from Detroit to Chicago, in many instances within a stone's throw of the Ottawa settlements. The weakness of the Greenville agreement was only too apparent.[23]

A case in point was the 1807 treaty negotiated at Detroit. Gravely concerned that certain Ottawa, Potawatomi, Chippewa, and Wyandot leaders who had visited Fort Malden near Detroit were contemplating a formal alliance with the British, Michigan Territorial Governor William Hull under authority of the War Department distributed money and goods aggregating $10,000 in exchange for an anti-British stance and a significant land cession in northwestern Ohio and southeastern Michigan. But the Roche de Boeuf Ottawas (and six other village groups) were able to have an article inserted that granted them specific reservations in the area, so long as the boundaries did not interfere with prior improvements of the whites. The option that some of the goods awarded could be issued in the form of implements of husbandry or domestic animals, and the provision for a blacksmith for a period of ten years, seemed to suggest that the Ottawas were relatively secure on their Ohio farms.

The Brownstone treaty the following year suggested otherwise. In a memo accompanying the official communication of the Detroit treaty to the Senate, President Jefferson emphasized that for strategic reasons and military security it was essential to obtain a right-of-way from the Connecticut Reserve in eastern Ohio to Fort Meigs on the Maumee River, less than ten miles north of the newly created Roche de Boeuf reserve. The Brownstone council accomplished precisely that. With Governor Hull negotiating at his finest, the Ottawas, Chippewas, Potawatomis, Wyandots, and Shawnees agreed to relinquish all claims to the fifty-mile trip suggested by Jefferson. In the final treaty language it was to be 120 feet wide, with one mile of land and all timber "on each side thereof" reserved for the purpose of establishing settlements. Short of outright cession of every acre in northern Ohio, no more efficient means could have been devised to guarantee quick white penetration of the entire region served by the road.[24]

The mounting Indian resistance that preceded the War of 1812 was equally disruptive to the Ottawas on the Maumee. It is difficult to gauge the number who actually participated in events that culminated in the military confrontation at Tippecanoe Creek in 1811 between forces led by General William Henry Harrison and the pan-Indian confederation led by the Shawnee Prophet and his brother Tecumseh. Considering their traditional anti-American attitude, the land-cession treaties that had diminished their ancient domain, their increasing problems with whiskey merchants, the destruction of their natural supply of game, and white encroachments in general, it is certain that at least some Ottawas were receptive to the teachings of the Prophet, whose nativistic doctrine denounced interracial marriages, alcohol, white clothing, private property, and the ways of the white man in general. The Prophet promised that in the Auglaize valley of northwest Ohio the specific means of salvation would be given to all believing Indians.

At Prophetstown on the lower Wabash a force estimated to have numbered well over a thousand Indians gathered in the summer of 1810. Nearly a dozen tribes were issued offensive assignments. While others were to attack such diverse points as Mackinac and Fort Dearborn in Michigan Territory and Fort Wayne and Vincennes in Indiana, the Ottawas and Chippewas were told to attack Detroit. Sporadic attacks did take place, and recruitment efforts were increased, but the only significant result more than a year later was the bloody battle with Harrison's forces on Tippecanoe Creek. Harrison reported a "decisive victory"; both sides suffered casualties numbering nearly two hundred; and while the Prophet's teachings fell into disrepute, and the Indians scattered to their respective villages, the importance of the confrontation was that it had taken place in what was to be the larger arena of the War of 1812. Once again the Ottawas and their relatives had been sucked into the mire of Anglo-American animosity.[25]

Those who fought Harrison came mainly from the ranks of the Potawatomis, Shawnees, Kickapoos, and Winnebagos —only a few Wyandots and Ottawas saw battle. Yet the latter were sympathetic to the Prophet's teaching promoting common ownership of Indian land as a strategy to block negotiations in which individual chiefs too often had been persuaded (often because of the influence or promise of alcohol) to cede lands for bribes and personal considerations. By 1812 the Maumee Ottawas had been sufficiently acculturated that they understood the futility of returning to the past, and their resiliency allowed them to take what they could from the white man while maintaining at least some basics of traditional village life. Still holding a common, though limited, land base, though literally hemmed in by the individualistic society of the invaders, they made efforts to renew old associations and the traditions of the past. In his journal of his service as United States Indian Agent at the Consolidated Mackinac and Sault Sainte Marie Agency, Henry R. Schoolcraft recorded the following conversation with Ossiganac, a L'Arbre Croche Ottawa, who had served as interpreter at the British post on Drummond Island:

> 6th [June 1834]. Ossiganac, at an interview at my house [in Mackinac] this afternoon, says that the Ottawas of Maumee, Ohio, sent a message to the Ottawas of L'Abre Croche [just south of Mackinac], in Governor Hull's time—consequently between 1805 and 1812—saying: "We were originally of one fire, and we wish to come back again to you, that we may all derive heat again from the same fire." The Ottawas of L'Abre Croche replied: "True, but you took a coal to warm yourselves by. Now, it will be better that your remain by your own coal, which you saw fit long ago to take from our fire. Remain where you are." From that day the Ottawas of Maumee have said nothing more about joining us.[26]

The War of 1812 obliterated whatever possibility there had been of an understanding between the Michigan and Ohio Ottawas or a more coordinated and practical challenge with the other Northwest tribes against the invading Americans. The Peace of Ghent, minus the British proposal for a neutral Indian state in the Northwest, was ratified by the Senate on February 15, 1815. Seven months later the same body ratified the Treaty of Spring Wells, which dealt with the united tribes who had been "associated with Great Britain in the late war between the United States and that power." Like the Potawatomis, Chippewas, Miamis, Shawnees, Delawares, and Senecas, the Ottawas agreed to resume formal relations with the United States, under the same conditions that had prevailed before the war, and to place themselves under the exclusive protection of the United States. No new land cessions were required, but it was clearly understood that all of the tribes would abide by all land cessions dating back to the Treaty of Greenville.[27]

The illusion of postwar stability was shattered by a new hoard of settlers imbued with such a nationalistic ferver as only the alleged victory over Britain could excite. They viewed themselves as the guardians and promoters of progress, and they brought pressure on the government to have all land titles cleared in Ohio. There was the added concern that the Indians of Ohio and Michigan were still too friendly to the British. By 1817 the War Department could no longer demur. Responding to directions from the White House, Acting Secretary of War George Graham instructed Michigan Territorial Governor Lewis Cass to make an effort to extinguish all Indian land titles in Ohio. Two basic strategies were outlined in Graham's memo to Cass:

> The negotiations should be founded on the basis that each head of a family who wishes to remain within the limits ceded should have a life estate in a reservation of certain number of acres, which should descend to his children in fee, reserving to the widow (if any) her thirds; and those who do not wish

to remain on those terms should have a body of land allotted to them west of the Mississippi.[28]

Cass and Duncan McArthur met with the Indians at Fort Meigs in late September and in short order secured the surrender of 3,880,320 acres in northwestern Ohio, southern Michigan, and northeastern Indiana. The Indians, including the Ottawas, received what the Indian Claims Commission more than a century later termed an unconscionable slight increase in annuities. But the most controversial aspect of the treaty was that it authorized that over a quarter million acres be granted in the form of individual and limited reserves patented in fee simple with unlimited powers of conveyance. Significantly, the Roche de Boeuf reserve remained intact, with continuing restrictions on alienation. A total of 21,760 acres, also inalienable, were granted to the Ottawa groups at the Blanchard's Fork of the Big Auglaize River and on the Little Auglaize (including Oquanoxie's village). "In the progress of our negotiations with the Indians," reported Cass and McArthur, "we have experienced much difficulty in adjusting the quantity, tenure, and conditions of the reservations to their and our satisfaction."

Admitting that they had taken their instructions from Washington as "rather advisory than imperative," the two commissioners emphasized that to have taken a different course of action would have been "fatal to our exertions and the expectations of the Government." While Graham was pleased with the massive cession, he voiced some concern over the compactness of some reserves, for example, that of the Ottawas, which in his view would "preserve their customs and manners for a longer period than if they had made their locations more diffusely." Congress, on the other hand, was more concerned about the privilege of allowing the recipients of individual reserves the absolute right of selling to whomever they desired—often the Indians sold to land speculators and traders to whom they were indebted. Consequently, the supplementary

Saint Mary's treaty negotiated in the fall of 1818 elimi-
nated the alienation clauses of the 1817 treaty. To have
done otherwise would have opened a Pandora's box of
future allotments in Ohio, Michigan, and Indiana that would
have endangered the very foundation of the government's
emerging removal policy. The supplementary treaty also
increased annuity payments to the Ottawas and three other
tribes.[29]

Traders, land jobbers, and public officials were not the
only ones who eyed the Indians' diminishing land base with
greed. While not directly related to land transactions in
northwest Ohio, article 16 of the 1817 treaty had established an important precedent for Indian education west
of the Mississippi. Reflecting what still was considered a
viable but faltering assimilationist solution to the Indian
problem, as well as the belief that education, civilization,
Christianity, and progress were inexorably intertwined,
Cass and McArthur had written a provision into the Fort
Meigs Treaty that granted in fee simple to the rector of
the Catholic Church of Saint Anne in Detroit and the
"corporation of the College of Detroit" a total of 2,560
acres. The justification was that some of the Ottawas,
Potawatomis, and Chippewas with a Catholic "attachment"
were interested in having schools provided for their children. The final decision concerning the location of these
lands was left to the superintendent of Indian affairs in
Michigan Territory, an office at that time held by Cass.
The provision constituted a significant commitment to tribal
education, and its implications for various denominations
interested in moving west did not go unnoticed.[30]

Before that time only a few schools had been established
in areas that the government considered to be Indian country, and in the absence of significant federal assistance they
remained dormant and had experienced little growth. In
August, 1819, Superintendent of the Indian Trade Thomas
L. McKenney reported only four in existence: a Cherokee
school operated in Brainard, Tennessee, by the American
Board of Foreign Missions; a much smaller Cherokee school

run by the Moravians; and two Quaker schools among the Senecas. These, plus a few "minor and fugitive" schools of unknown sponsorship located outside of Indian country, were all there were on the official list before the grant to the Catholics in Detroit.

Like Cass, Superintendent McKenney became increasingly vocal in support of Indian education once it became apparent that the assimilationist program was faltering and that the vast lands of the trans-Mississippi West were ideally suited for the funding of schools. In McKenney's view it was absolutely essential that schools be established alongside the fields, workshops, and houses provided by the government, so that the moral could complement the practical.

Significant support for that approach came from Congressman Henry Southard, who headed a House committee that had been given responsibility for responding to President Monroe's 1818 message on Indian affairs. Prefacing his remarks with a summary of the uncertain state of the Indian trade and the unmet needs of the Indians, Southard made a special plea for education as a civilizing force. As a guideline he noted the unusual accomplishments of schools sponsored by missionary and benevolent societies among the Hottentots of South Africa and the Hindus of India. Thousands of these backward people had "yielded to instruction," and many more awaited the attention of philanthropy. Here in America, however, the advantage of not having to translate books and the Bible into some exotic language had gone largely unnoticed. Indeed, the need was simply to establish English schools among the tribes where moral instruction could be mixed with hard work. "Put into the hands of their children the primer and the hoe," said Southard, "and, as their minds become enlightened and expand, the Bible will be their book; and they will grow up in habits of morality and industry, leave the chase to those whose minds are less cultivated, and become useful members of society."[31]

Arguments of that sort and certain evidence that, as the

Indians were increasingly hemmed in by white settlers, their progress toward "civilization" was being thwarted and even reversed, resulted in the passage, on March 3, 1819, of an "Act making provision for the civilization of the Indian tribes adjoining the frontier settlements." A modest annual appropriation of $10,000 was to be used as the president saw fit, the official objects being to improve the moral character of the Indians, to instruct them in agricultural techniques, and to teach their children the fundamentals of reading, writing, and arithmetic.[32] Meanwhile, the assault on tribal land continued. So long as the government's assimilationist strategy had remained intact, the Ottawa reserves on the Maumee had remained relatively secure, though there is little evidence that their inhabitants were progressing toward the prescribed level of civilization. In the early 1820s, however, a greater threat came from southern Michigan and northern Indiana on the west. After extensive preparations by Governor Cass and a Michigan politician named Solomon Sibley, a large delegation of Potawatomi, Ottawa, and Chippewa leaders were assembled at Chicago in August, 1821. The site was selected so that the land the Indians were being asked to relinquish would not be in direct view and thus remind them of the past. The Ottawas and Chippewas agreed to a cession encompassing the southwestern quarter of the future state of Michigan, and an eleven-mile strip on the northern border of Indiana. They were promised increased annuities; limited reserves carved out of land ceded, which could be held by the Indians until purchased by the whites; and a plentiful supply of whiskey once the negotiations were completed. The obstructionism of a Potawatomi minority led by Metea (Mee-te-ay) was effectively neutralized by pleas by the Ottawa and Chippewa delegations, pressure from trader and mixed-blood members of all three tribes, and the promise of more whiskey once the treaty had been signed. "We care not for the land, the money or the goods," pleaded one elderly Potawatomi, "it is the whiskey we want—give us the whiskey." Metea and his followers finally capitulated, and within twenty-four hours nearly a dozen Indians had died from excessive drinking. The treaty signed August 29, 1821, and proclaimed the following March 25, reserved five tracts for village groups and twenty-six individual, but not fee-simple, grants. Thus by the spring of 1822 the Maumee and Auglaize Ottawas were virtually surrounded either by white settlements or land greatly coveted by the invader. Eight years later, after the government had committed itself formally to a removal policy, Superintendent McKenney admitted to Secretary of War John Eaton that about all the Northwest Indians could then do was "to catch fish—and plant patches of corn; dance, paint, hunt, fight, get drunk when they [could] get liquor, and often starve." Assimilation had failed, and the white disciples of civilized education looked for a more certain plan for saving the Ottawas.[33]

3

Providence and Removal

WRITING IN 1833 from the Baptist Missionary Rooms in Boston to the Reverend Isaac McCoy, who was busy surveying Indian reservations southwest of the Missouri River, the Reverend L. Bolles advised, "I may, however, say in a word, we are disposed to concentrate so far as Providence recommends, our forces in what I will call *The Indian Country.*" His statement was evidence that the missionary arm of the increasingly powerful Baptist denomination had determined to take advantage of a major change in United States Indian policy that had its roots in the Louisiana Purchase of 1803 and the Jeffersonian design for saving the eastern Indians from extinction.[1]

The Jeffersonian strategy for incorporating Indians into the mainstream of white American society had as one of its principal tactics the removal of Indians from the pernicious influences of the American frontier. Much friction had characterized Indian-white relations east of the Mississippi, and as President Jefferson designed a constitutional amendment to mitigate his ideological concern over the constitutionality of the Louisiana transaction, he gave close attention to the positive effect it might possibly have on Indians. He concluded that the area of Louisiana north of the thirty-first parallel was well suited to the needs of the Indians, whose removal from the East would allow for a greater concentration of the white population while at the same time protecting the Indians from negative conditioning by uncouth frontiersmen. The amendment, of course, proved unnecessary, but on the Indian question it told much about the inception of the removal policy that became more fashionable in the decade of the 1820s. Indeed, its basic argument foreshadowed the position of President Andrew Jackson, who in his first annual message to Congress in 1829, stated, "Surrounded by the whites with their arts of civilization, which by destroying the resources of the savage doom him to weakness and decay, the fate of the Mohegan, the Narragansett, and the Delaware is fast overtaking the Choctaw, the Cherokee, and the Creek." Jackson urged that if a region were provided west of the Mississippi for Indian resettlement—a place where the benevolent could teach the arts of civilization—the Indians would "raise up an interesting commonwealth, destined to perpetuate the race and attest [to] the humanity and justice of Government."[2] Ironically, despite all the philanthropic solicitude expressed by the policy makers, removal west implied destruction of the Indians' traditional cultures.

Between the Jefferson and Jackson administrations, paralleling the Ohio cession and various concentration treaties following the War of 1812, the government's assimilationist policy became increasingly unpopular. Some proponents of assimilation doggedly maintained that Indian decline could be reversed by a more stringent enforcement of the factory system of trade, more concentrated reserves, accelerated missionary activity, and even model Indian communities. Chief advocate of the latter was the Congregational minister Jedidiah Morse, who in 1820 was commissioned by the Reverent Society of Scotland and the Secretary of War, John C. Calhoun, to study conditions in the Indian country. His *Report*, released in 1822, was a strong and passionate appeal for the establishment of model Indian communities—communities composed of education "families" administered by ministers of the gospel.

Day-to-day operations were to be conducted by farmers, teachers, blacksmiths, millwrights, and carpenters. Women would instruct their native counterparts in the arts of cooking and sewing. These communities would be located not in remote areas of the frontier but in fertile, well-established centers of Indian-white contact. Each would have its own churches and schools, and eventually there would be a centrally located college for all. "Let this College be liberally endowed," said Morse, "out of the avails of those public lands which have been purchased [from] the Indians. To what better purpose can a portion of them be applied?" Concerning the offspring of Indian-white marriages—an ever-increasing phenomenon in the Indian country—Morse was especially optimistic, saying, "They only require *education*, and the enjoyment of our privileges, to make them a valuable portion of our citizens." Such limited removal as might take place, cautioned Morse, should only be the removal of small or remnant tribes to the main centers of Indian population.[3]

Nonetheless, some public officials viewed blanket removal as virtually inevitable. The land base of the Indians, while greatly diminished, was a powerful attraction both to land speculators and white settlers, and it was difficult to ignore those tribes who held strategically located reserves or who were otherwise in a position to defy the states and the federal government on constitutional or purely diplomatic grounds. On January 6, 1820, less than a year after the Civilization Bill providing government support for Indian education had passed, Congress instructed the War Department to report on the progress made in the civilization of Indian tribes and the sums of money that had been expended for that purpose. Nine days later War Secretary John C. Calhoun reported that none of the $10,000 appropriated in 1819 for that purpose had been expended, principally because the president was in the process of identifying benevolent individuals and societies who could best carry out the work with zeal and efficiency. The secretary went on to identify certain tribes

who had made considerable progress—principally the
southern Indians and remnants of the Six Nations—and the
successes that schools sponsored by missionary groups were
experiencing. Yet Calhoun was basically pessimistic and
called for change:

> Although partial advance may be made under the present sys-
> tem to civilize the Indians [maintaining schools adjacent to
> white settlements], I am of the opinion that, until there is a
> radical change in the system, any efforts which may be made
> must fall short of complete success. They must be brought
> gradually under our authority and laws, or they will insensibly
> waste away on vice and misery. It is impossible, with their
> customs, that they should exist as independent communities
> in the midst of civilized society.[4]

As pressure mounted in favor of removal, the churches
and missionary societies joined in the debate. On the one
hand, they were reluctant to abandon those missions and
schools fairly well established in the East, but on the other,
they were realistic enough to realize the difficulties involved in preventing further settler and speculator encroachment. In any case, they saw the government civilization fund as a proper means of increasing their benevolent
activities, whether in the East or in some western Indian
colony. They believed that Christianity, particularly Protestantism, was inextricably a part of civilization, and that
civilization meant progress. Coupled with Christian ideal-
ism, their formula for improvement was imbued with in-
dividualism as a component of any institutional arrangement. They were urged on by the notion of a unilinear
development that placed the American nation at the pin-
nacle of western civilization. Buttressed by such a meta-
physical assurance, frontier missionaries could not rest until
their conception of reality had taken hold in the western
wilderness in general and among the unfortunate Indians
in particular. They assumed that such a noble undertaking
deserved the financial support of the nation. Representa-

tives of the American Board of Foreign Missions for Pecuniary Aid in Civilizing Indians told Congress in 1824:

> The work in which we are engaged, we are sensible, is not only noble and godlike, and worthy to command the best energies of our nature, but it is also a great, arduous, and difficult work, requiring patience, forbearance, perseverance, and unremitted and long-continued efforts. Here is scope enough to employ the wisdom, the *means* [emphasis added], and the power of the nation; and the object is of sufficient magnitude and interest to command the employment of them all.[5]

The Baptists, soon to figure so heavily in the destiny of the Ohio Ottawas, displayed flexibility regarding *where* the good work could best be performed. In 1822, for example, an Indian missions committee of the Baptist Home Mission Board reported that self-sustaining Indian settlements cooperating with white farmers and merchants in the worship of God were "anticipated [in] a period not far distant." At the same time it was essential "to carry the gospel and the blessings of civilized life to the dark and distant regions of the west, until the rocky mountains shall resound with harmony and praise and the shores of the Pacific shall be the only boundary of this wide sweep of human civilization and Christian benevolence." In short, the work could and must be carried on wherever the Indians were.[6]

Just as Protestantism was considered the very essence of civilization, so education was seen as the one most powerful tool for raising the savage to the high level of white culture. Indeed, in the view of most public officials and church leaders, the two were virtually synonymous. Education was considered to be essential for breaking down the language barrier; for making the gospel intelligible to the heathen mind; for instruction in the agricultural, mechanical, and domestic arts; and for making the Indian a virtuous person. Especially important was the training of native missionaries who could carry on the civilizing program in areas where missionaries were less effective or simply not welcome.

In an 1824 memorial to Congress, John Cotton Smith, Jonas Platt, Jedidiah Morse, Stephan Van Rensselaer, and Jeremiah Evarts specifically called for the establishment of two core Indian colleges for the instruction of promising native missionaries. To them such colleges were indispensable to the success of the civilization program that had already been inaugurated by concerned Christiandom. Once a northern and southern Indian college were firmly established, those institutions would "form the rudiments of future towns and cities, and even states, and ultimately civilization itself." Funding for this noble activity posed no problem whatsoever: "A very small part of the profits on the many millions of acres of most valuable lands purchased by the Government of these [eastern] Indians would furnish pecuniary means for the support of as many educational establishments as would be competent to the purpose."⁷

The assumed sale of such a massive quantity of Indian land indicated that the pendulum of philanthropic sentiment was swinging in favor of removal. As civilization monies were distributed to the various church groups, Congress displayed concern whether the results justified further funding; some went so far as to question whether the Civilization Act should not be repealed in its entirety. Congressman William McLean of Ohio, for example, representing the House Committee on Indian Affairs and responding to a House resolution calling for an inquiry into repealing the 1819 Act, reported that the twenty-three schools in existence in 1824 were thriving and that the wish of the Indians to have their children educated was so urgent that numerous applications were being refused simply because of the limited means that the schools possessed. With the exception of three fledgling schools in Missouri and Arkansas (one with no students yet enrolled), all were located east of the Mississippi and were receiving substantial nongovernment support for their operations. "But," cautioned McLean, "the Committee are well persuaded that, had the Government afforded no pecuniary aid, very few, if any, of the benefits which have been conferred, would have been experienced by the Indians." As to removal, McLean was noticeably reticent. About all he could say was that the Indians had partaken more of white vices than virtues, and that in their present condition they had to be civilized or exterminated. No other alternative existed.[8] Less equivocating on removal was Thomas H. Benton of Missouri, a powerful member of the Senate Committee on Indian Affairs and a spokesman for a frontier state with its fair share of Indian population. Encouraged that even the most ardent supporters of assimilation realized that close contact with white society often had deleterious effects on the Indians, Senator Benton (with the strong support of the Missouri General Assembly) made a strong case for removal. In no uncertain terms he insisted:

> The experience of centuries has shown that Indian tribes, placed in small masses, in the midst of a white population, are constantly exposed to the influence of causes which operate to the degradation of their character, and to the diminution of their numbers. The contact of two races of people, differing in language and character, in which the weaker party are most usually the sufferers, both in the first wrong, and in the final punishment. To the State itself, the existence of separate communities within its bosom, and independent of its laws, is a palpable evil, an anomaly in government, and a direct inconsistency with the policy and jurisdiction of a sovereign State.[9]

Benton suggested that the area west of Missouri and Arkansas Territory, which in his view was only "nominally" owned by the Osage and Kansa nations, was an ideal place for the eastern tribes. He saw no difficulty in arranging a cession approximately 100 to 200 miles wide between the Red River and the Missouri for the emigrant Indians, with the Osages and Kansas retaining suitable portions for themselves. Understandably, he was especially anxious to remove Indians from his own state, since they had "suffered too much from the contact and pressure of white population."[10] A year later a substantial part of Benton's recommendation had been realized. In early June, 1825, Indian Superintendent William Clark met with the Osage and Kansa leadership in Saint Louis and succeeded in negotiating two massive land cession treaties which broke the land barrier to an emerging removal plan for Indians east of the Mississippi.[11]

During the next five years the debate over a workable removal policy intensified. Responding to a report of Secretary of War Calhoun dated January 24, 1824, which summarized data regarding the number of Indians east of the Mississippi, their land holdings, their progress in white education, and the anticipated costs of removal, President James Monroe dispatched a removal plan to the Senate—one that would prevent further crises among the states, the settlers, and the Indians while at the same time assuring political and humanitarian institutions once the Indians had been relocated in the west. The constitutional crisis between the Cherokee Nation and Georgia in 1831-32 was, of course, instrumental in the actual expulsion of the eastern Indians, but the conversion of Indian Trade Superintendent Thomas McKenney to a removal philosophy was especially comforting to the antiassimilationists.

McKenney, whose attempt at bringing missionary activity under government regulation had met with little success, had been concerned about mixed-blood opposition to removal, but he became a firm supporter of removal once he had completed a tour of the Indian country in 1827. After a trip that took him from Washington, D.C., to Green Bay and then to the Five Civilized Tribes in the South, he concluded that the wretched circumstances he had observed made removal the only realistic alternative to extinction. In Washington, however, McKenney faced strong congressional opposition from New England, the Middle Atlantic states, and the upper South—areas with little or no Indian population. Missionaries well established with particular tribes were influential in holding the line, as was the powerful American Board of Foreign Missions in New York. Finally, in the spring of 1828, McKenney obtained a $15,000 appropriation for sending government officials to explore the western country as a possible place for future Indian residence. This appropriation provided the financial means and government authority for the Reverend Isaac McCoy to become directly involved in the removal of Indians from the old Northwest to the area west of Missouri, and the eventual establishment of an Ottawa Baptist mission and educational facility in the future state of Kansas.[12]

Until government assistance became available through the Civilization Act of 1819, missionary activity among the Ottawas had been limited to the work of the Roman Catholic Church. Alternatively known as the Ottawa or the Huron mission of the upper Great Lakes, the Catholic attempt to convert Indians included Chippewas, Potawatomis, refugee Hurons, Menominees, Winnebagos, Sauks, Foxes, and Mississippi River Sioux as well. Following the pioneering work of Jean de Brébeuf, S. J., among the Hurons in 1634 and additional efforts among the Chippewas at Sault Sainte Marie in 1641, the Jesuit Felix Ménard said the first mass on the banks of Keweenaw Bay in 1660. A year later he lost his life at a portage and thus became the first martyr of the Catholic mission. In 1664, Father Claude Allouez spoke on the subject of paradise and hell and other "mysteries" to a group of sixty Ottawas at Montreal. "They paid excellent attention," reported Allouez, "listening to me in greater silence than when their Captain harangued them." The following year he constructed a small chapel of bark on the western shore of Chequamegon Bay — which came to be known as the La Pointe Mission. Yet it was difficult to contend with the Indians' traditions. "There is here a false and abdominable religion," complained Allouez in 1666, "resembling in many respects the beliefs of some of the ancient pagans. The Savages of these regions recognize no sovereign master of Heaven and Earth, but believe there are many spirits." Three years later it was reported that Father Allouez had refused to return to the Ottawas because of their "superstitions" and

extraordinary dedication to "feasts and juggleries."[13]
Greater success was experienced at the Saint Joseph
Mission in the Saint Joseph River valley near present Niles,
Michigan. Following the Iroquois raids of the midseven-
teenth century, many Algonquian people returned to the
southern Michigan peninsula, where the Saint Joseph Mission had been established in the late 1670s or early 1680s.
A specific grant for what then was called the Ottawa Mission was recorded in 1686. Father Allouez served there
until his death in 1689. His successors were Fathers Claude
Aveneau (1689–1698), Jean Mermet (1698–1702), and
Jean Baptiste Chardon (1702–1712). For the next seven
or eight years there were no resident missionaries at Saint
Joseph. In 1720, Father Michel Guignas arrived, only to
find that a group of traders and brandy merchants had established themselves in the vicinity. Efforts to control the
liquor traffic were met with Indian threats to turn to the
English for a regular supply. Defections became commonplace, so that by the middle of the eighteenth century the
mission was anything but thriving. The last recorded
Catholic baptism was that of "[M]arianne, " a forty-five-
year-old Ottawa woman in April 22, 1752. The protracted
French war with Britain and the secularization of the Jesuits
by the French government in 1762, which was implemented at Saint Joseph on July 3, 1763, sealed the doom of
the mission, which then was known simply as Fort Saint
Joseph. It was at this site that the Baptists under the guidance of Isaac McCoy established the Carey Mission more
than half a century later.[14]
Few individuals were better suited than Isaac McCoy to
attempt to fuse providence, progress, and Christianity into
a practical program for Indian "civilization." Born in Union-
town, Pennsylvania, in 1784 and raised on the Kentucky
frontier, McCoy was ordained a Baptist minister in 1810.
Seven years later he was sent by the Baptist Board of
Foreign Missions to a Miami village on the middle Wabash
River, about sixteen miles north of Terre Haute. Frustrated
in his attempts to obtain permission for a permanent mis-

sion from either the government or the Miamis, McCoy purchased a small tract near the Wea reserve on nearby Racoon Creek, where he constructed a cabin for his family and a school for the Indians and nearby white settlers. Difficulties there, and difficulties with the Baptist headquarters in Boston over excessive administrative interference in Indian country, were tempered by the passage of the Civilization Act, which had the potential to fund McCoy's developing dream of an Indian Canaan west of the Mississippi. Yet his subsequent efforts among the Miamis and Potawatomis at Fort Wayne did not attract government backing. Instead, the meager support extended the Baptists at this time went to Richard M. Johnson's school at Great Crossings, Kentucky, and to the Reverend John Peck's Hamilton Mission among the Oneidas in New York.[15]

A personal visit to Washington, D.C., and an audience with Secretary Calhoun in late 1821, plus the increasing confidence McCoy came to enjoy from Superintendent Lewis Cass in Michigan, resulted in McCoy's appointment in the summer of 1822 as official teacher to the Potawatomis and superintendent of "Civilization Programs" for both the Potawatomis and the Ottawas. A Presbyterian mission among the nearby Maumee Ottawas had received some modest government assistance, but apparently had failed. Thus McCoy and his frontier Baptist followers, armed with a federal appropriation that in 1824 amounted to $600 per year, were able to take over where the Catholic fathers had abandoned the field more than half a century earlier. McCoy named the new station Carey Mission, which was not far from the site of old Fort Saint Joseph, after William Carey, the prominent Baptist missionary in Serampore, India. In 1824, McCoy proudly reported that Carey was "prosperous and increasing" and that Thomas Mission had been established for the Ottawas as an "appendage" of Carey on the Grand River about eighty-five miles north. The dual missions served as a training ground and as the institutional link between the Baptist activities in Michigan and northern Ohio and the future operations among the Maumee Ottawas in Kansas.[16] Despite McCoy's official optimism, efforts to effect positive change among the Ottawas and the other peninsular tribes met with significant obstacles—obstacles that only fortified his belief that removal was the only practical course. Repeated land dispossession treaties had reduced many of the Indians to a dependency on annuities and the alcohol these funds provided. The sharp practices of traders, who knew only too well how to work through government commissioners and frustrated tribal leaders, kept the tribes chronically in debt. Land jobbers and their squatter retainers kept pressuring the War Department and Congress for more of the land that the Indians seemed unable to cultivate or develop, and the language barrier dictated that more time was needed to establish meaningful communication for moral improvement and gospel teaching. Added to this was the renewal of Catholic mission activity, which seemed to have as its objective the elimination of the Baptists from the Indian country of Michigan, Ohio and Indiana. Based on his experiences with an unidentified Catholic priest at Fort Wayne, McCoy recalled,

> His subject was Baptism, and his discourse was mainly directed against Baptist sentiment. I soon became convinced that his design was to provoke altercation with me, which he might, through the Catholics mingling with the Indians, turn to the disadvantage of our mission. I have been admonished by their prejudices, soon after I became a missionary, to be ever on the alert in regard to them.[17]

The Reverend Leonard Slater, McCoy's missionary assistant at Thomas, experienced particular pressure at the hands of the Catholics, who renewed their mission efforts in the Grand River area in the early 1830s. Following a summary of the Ottawas' historical preference for Catholic dogma, Father Frederick Baraga asserted somewhat sarcastically:

The [Baptist] non-Catholics, with their inexhaustible means, cannot make any considerable gain among the Indians. A striking example of this may be seen in the place where I baptized the forty-six savages. A Protestant minister [Slater] undertook the task of gaining the savages for his doctrine. He has spent almost nine years there and is being amply supported by his co-religionists. Besides the $400.00 paid as an annual salary, provisions, and clothing are sent him, but with all these means he has been able in nine years to convert only ten Indians. On the other hand, a Catholic priest, poor and despoiled of all temporal goods but well supplied with treasures of truth and salvation, not only completely won over forty-six in the same place, but many others promised to accept the Catholic religion as soon as he could come again to stay with them permanently.[18]

From the Baptist perspective the situation at Carey was not much better. Robert Simerwell, a pious blacksmith who was left in charge during one of McCoy's many absences, wrote McCoy in 1832: "I am opposed in every attempt to do anything at this place by an unprincipled subagent. . . . The Indians are drinking in catholicism very fast. Pacagin [an Ottawa leader] has become a preacher of that doctrine. . . . God only knows what will happen to this mission."[19]

Superintendent McKenney's flexibility and his acquiescence toward removal were encouraging to McCoy. Shortly before his fact-finding tour of the Indian country, McKenney had written a memo to Secretary of War James Barbour on the subject of schools, their Christian sponsors, and a possible removal policy. Noting that all teachers save one Methodist among the Ohio Wyandots favored removal, McKenney emphasized the widespread concern over the financial losses in buildings and permanent equipment that would have to be abandoned once the Indians had been removed. "But when these objections are answered in the further development of the plan," said McKenney, "and that the money they had laid out where they now are would doubtless be reimbursed . . . they were satisfied with the measure." Then, in a direct reference to McCoy, the head of the Indian Office reported that "in one instance a proposition has been made by a teacher to go and explore the country, and open the way for the removal of the Indians who are particularly within his charge."[20] This was the immediate background to McCoy's appointment as treasurer of the western exploration commission created by the 1828 legislation and was indicative of his (and the Baptists') increasing influence in Indian affairs. The commission also included George H. Kennerly, nephew of Saint Louis Indian Superintendent William Clark, and George P. Todson, whose knowledge of diseases peculiar to the West qualified him for the position. McKenney arranged for representatives of the Chickasaws and Choctaws to accompany the expedition. For his part, McCoy brought three Potawatomis and three Ottawas, the latter apparently without official authorization. In Saint Louis in early August, 1828, while waiting for the arrival of the southern Indians, McCoy took time to compose a more detailed plan for his Indian Canaan, which he envisioned as a place where with the help of the government, the Ottawas, Potawatomis, Chippewas, Miamis, and "others" would finally secure benefits from the white man's benevolence.[21]

The general area selected by McCoy (in consultation with Clark) was between the Arkansas Territory and Missouri on the one side and the Rocky Mountains and Mexico on the other. He noted the residence of at least six tribes in that vast region, but because they lacked "permanency," the civilization program was not to apply to them at that time. Within the confines of this vast region a specific country should be set aside for the eastern Indians that would be their exclusive property. Politically, the area should have a government comparable to those of territories of the United States. Counties and county seats including one or two tribes should be organized, with persons of Indian extraction holding office as associate judges, clerks, and sheriffs—all paid by the federal government and administered by agents or subagents appointed to each tribe. A central site should be selected for a pan-Indian metropolis that would serve as a territorial capitol and common Indian meetingplace, where the presence of a governor, a secretary, an attorney, and a territorial judge appointed by the president would place this western Canaan on a par with the rest of the United States. Finally, McCoy contemplated a comprehensive plan of education to be funded either by treaties or congressional appropriations, presumably to be administered by the various Christian denominations.[22]

Leaving Saint Louis in late August, McCoy traveled in a southwesterly direction to the struggling Harmony Mission operated by the American Board of Commissioners for Foreign Missions on the Marais des Cygnes, or Osage, River near the western border of Missouri. From there he and his Indian companions traveled up the Marais des Cygnes to a point where the river intersected the Santa Fe Trail. From there they moved north to the upper Neosho River watershed, to the Mission Creek village of the Kansa tribe, just west of present-day Topeka, and then back to Saint Louis. The trip, which took the party directly across the future site of the Ottawa Indian University, took forty-nine days and was accomplished without major incident, largely because McCoy stayed away from settlements where the Indians might have obtained liquor. McCoy was impressed with the richness of the soil and the abundance of game in the rolling countryside. While the Indians generally agreed, they did "lament the scarcity of wood, and especially the almost total absence of the sugar tree."[23]

From that time onward McCoy disassociated himself from the floundering Carey and Thomas missions and devoted most of his time to lobbying for a removal bill, conducting additional explorations and surveying missions for the government, and establishing himself with other Baptists on the Missouri frontier. There they would be in a more strategic position to relocate the anticipated Baptist Indian settlement in the West. Early in 1829, McCoy wrote to Congressman William McLean that little difficulty was anticipated in removing at least portions of the Ottawas, Potawatomis, and Miamis to what he now called "the new

Indian Territory." From his home in Fayette, Missouri, he wrote Governor Cass that he and other Baptist leaders were getting ready to move to the "Indian Canaan." "We suppose," said McCoy, "that a year from this time we will [be] nearly or quite close to closing our labors in Michigan." And to Congress, on behalf of a group of Baptist memorialists, he called attention to a specific site on the Marais des Cygnes, about fifty miles west of Missouri, that was ideally suited for the relocation of the Michigan missions and the construction of a centralized town, "from which should emanate the instructions of the United States to all parts of the [Indian] Territory." In short, McCoy was hopeful of making a Baptist school, mission, and political center the focal point of the entire Indian country.[24]

In McCoy's absence the situation at Carey was anything but favorable. On September 20, 1828, the Saint Joseph Potawatomis negotiated a treaty that relinquished additional land in southwest Michigan and northern Indiana, but said nothing about removal. Article 5 of the treaty provided a means whereby the Baptists could be compensated for their buildings and other improvements, should they decide to relocate west of the Mississippi, but that provision was compromised by an important disclaimer: "But, as the location is upon the [Saint Joseph] Indian reservation, the Commissioners are unwilling to assume the responsibility, of making this provision absolute, and therefore its rejection is not to affect any other part of the treaty." In other words, neither the federal commissioners, Lewis Cass and Pierre Menard, nor the Potawatomis were prepared to make removal or compensation for the Baptists at Carey and Thomas a condition of the important land cessions involved.[25]

More encouraging was the situation among the Ottawas. Whether the three Ottawas who accompanied McCoy on the 1828 journey to the future Kansas Territory came from the Saint Joseph or the Maumee area is difficult to determine. In any case, their message to President Jackson early in 1829 was instrumental in the Baptist decision to

cast their lot with the Ottawas. With a good deal of prompt-
ing on the part of McCoy and the Baptist leadership, no
less than six Ottawa leaders petitioned Jackson:

> Two of us whose names occur below accompanied Mr. McCoy
> on the late exploring expedition west of Missouri. . . . We
> have been informed that Mr. McCoy and Mr. [Johnston] Lykins
> with others of their missionary associates, propose settling in
> the country west of the state of Missouri, together with many
> of the tall pupils of their schools, some of whom belong to
> our tribe. We therefore pray our Great Father the President,
> to contemplate residence. We ask leave to go thither with a
> view of making that our residence, and we shall be thankful
> for whatever assistance in our removal and on our arrival in
> the new country [is received from] the kindness of our Great
> Father. We further ask for similar indulgence for such others
> of our tribe as shall choose to accompany us and to avail them-
> selves of such favours.[26]

Requests of this sort were encouraging to President Jackson, who made Indian relocation an important aspect of his
first administrative program. In his annual message to Congress in December, 1829, the president emphasized that
unless the Indians were moved to an area west of the Mississippi (where it was hoped that they would go voluntarily), they would only be further degraded and ultimately
ruined. Legally, their position was untenable, since to remain in the East was tantamount to submission to state
authority; the constitution simply did not allow Indian
states to be organized and administered within the boundaries of existing states. A Senate removal bill providing
permanent ownership of new lands, payment for ceded
lands, and financial assistance for actual emigration was
fiercely debated, with a number of church groups opposed.
In contrast to the more powerful American Board of Commissioners for Foreign Missions, which did its utmost to
block the bill, the Baptists were divided on the issue.
McCoy, who had gone to Washington in November, 1829,
served as principal lobbyist for the removal faction, while

the Baptist central missionary headquarters in Boston was much less zealous in support of Jackson. The removal bill finally passed by a close margin and was signed into law on May 28, 1830. With guarded optimism McCoy wrote to his son: "I cannot, of course, say whether anything will be done for us, or to promote our particular views or not. I am, of course, doing all in my power."[27]

As in other areas with substantial pockets of Indian population, the white settlers in the Maumee valley applauded the removal bill. The completion of the Erie Canal in 1825 had greatly stimulated the white advance into northern Ohio, and many believed that traders' claims against the Ottawas would soon equal the actual market value of the Maumee reservation. Moreover, it was the white sentiment, the several strategically located Ottawa tracts devalued adjacent white lands and inhibited the commercial development of the Maumee watershed. On August 2, 1830, a group of settlers and land speculators dispatched a petition to Indian Superintendent Cass, which read in part:

> We the undersigned residing in the Southern Section of the [Michigan] Territory, being naturally affected in our interest and convenience by the possession of the Ottoway tribe of Indians of large tracts of land on both sides of the mouth of the Maumee River, the peculiarity of the situation on their lands is such, that their being held by the Indians keeps other large tracts and important situations from being improved. In short, in relation to the people of the country, it is the key to the river. A law having been passed for the purchasing or exchanging of lands with the Indians, and their removal, we have conceived that you are or probably will be vested with power of the negotiations with Indians for this purpose. . . . We are not alone anxious for the removal of them. The State of Ohio as a state, is very solicitous, and the whole of the Northern line of the state are particularly anxious for the removal of these Indians from the reservations they now hold.[28]

Similar pressure coming from other parts of Ohio resulted in the appointment of James B. Gardiner as a special United States commissioner for Indian removal. On the pattern of Secretary of War John H. Eaton's negotiations with the Choctaws at Dancing Rabbit Creek in September, 1830, Gardiner concluded cession and removal treaties with the Sandusky Senecas on February 28, 1831; with the Lewiston and Great Miami Senecas and Shawnees the following July 20; and with the Wapaghkonnetta and Hog Creek Shawnees on August 8. On August 30, 1831, at the foot of the Maumee rapids just southwest of present-day Toledo, he concluded a land-cession and removal treaty with the Blanchard's Fork, Oquanoxie, and Roche de Boeuf Ottawas.[29]

Far more acceptable to McCoy and the Baptists than the 1828 negotiations with the Saint Joseph Potawatomis, this Ottawa treaty was obviously the result of hard bargaining on all sides, and, from the perspective of the proponents of an immediate Indian Canaan in the West, it was a mixed bag of blessings. All three Ottawa groups ceded the Ohio lands that they had been awarded by the treaties of 1807 and 1817. The treaty included careful stipulations for the public disposal of those lands and arrangements for the payment of the massive debts that the Ottawas owed local traders. Subsistence monies were authorized for removal. The Blanchard's Fork and Oquanoxie groups were granted 34,000 acres of land on "the western side of the Mississippi," while the Roche de Boeuf group was awarded 40,000 acres in the same general area. Yet no specific date for the actual removal of the first two groups was stipulated, and it was understood that if the Roche de Boeuf Ottawas wished not to emigrate immediately they could in fact defer removal so long as they did not take formal possession of their trans-Mississippi reserve. In short, the Indians had simply agreed to dispose of their Ohio lands in return for more acreage in the future Kansas, agricultural supplies, continued annuities, and considerable flexibility about precisely *when* they would emigrate. Yet, as it turned out, the settlement was a hollow victory for the

Indians. What remained, of course, was for the whiskey merchants, the land jobbers, and various white creditors to encumber the Ottawas' newly gained subsistence to such a degree that there would be no alternative but to move. Then, and only then, would McCoy's plan for an Indian Canaan and Ottawa survival be realized.[30]

In the meantime McCoy wrote to Secretary Eaton, requesting permission to transfer at government expense the Carey Mission and its students to a new school to be located west of Missouri "on the Osage [Marias des Cygnes] river." This brought no response, probably because some of McCoy's former student missionaries, especially the Reverend Leonard Slater, were opposed to removal. There also were significant differences over the virtues of boarding schools as opposed to village day schools, with McCoy favoring the former and the Carey Baptists preferring the latter.

On a more positive note, the War Department awarded McCoy some contracts to survey reservations for the eastern tribes who soon would emigrate to the western country. With his two sons, both of whom had taken formal instruction in surveying techniques, McCoy established himself on a small farm on the western border of Missouri and proceeded to select the various reserves. Since his superiors allowed him considerable discretion, it was hardly surprising that he placed the Blanchard's Fork and Oquanoxie Ottawas in an area bisected by the Marais des Cygnes River about thirty miles west of the Missouri boundary—in the very area that had so favorably impressed him during his exploring expedition in 1828.

To fulfill his dream of an Indian state, McCoy secured government authority to locate a six-mile-square section immediately south of the proposed Ottawa reservation where the political center for all the emigrant tribes might be located. This Indian capital would include an intertribal council house, a large grazing area for the ponies of visiting Indian dignitar es, and ample space for the development of an Indian town. McCoy also envisioned the establishment of an Indian university, and Indian printing press and newspaper, and other accouterments of a pan-Indian state. The obstacles were many, however, including the presence of government agents in the Indian country who were "inimical to missionary operations," competition from other missionary groups who were maneuvering for control of the government's civilization funds, and the failure to include a proposal for a formal Indian Territory and Indian seat of government in the Trade and Intercourse Act of 1834.[31]

On July 26, 1832, McCoy's son John, with two assistants, set out from the present-day Kansas City area to survey the 34,000-acre Ottawa reservation on the Marais des Cygnes. They completed their work on August 6. Less than four months later, on November 30, seventy-three Ottawas from Blanchard's Fork and Oquanoxie's village arrived at the Delaware and Shawnee Agency, which was then administered by United States Indian Agent Richard W. Cummins from a point about seven miles south of the mouth of the Kansas River. There the Baptists had established the Shawnee Baptist Mission to compete with the Methodists. The Ottawas' journey to the future Kansas Territory was directed by Lieutenant James J. Abert and G. W. Pool and accomplished with a minimum of difficulty. Traveling on horseback and by wagon from the Maumee River to Dayton, the Indians boarded canalboats for the trip to Cincinnati, where they changed to steamboats for the final leg of the journey to Westport Landing at the mouth of the Kansas River. Internal bickering, fear of what lay ahead, and an ample supply of alcohol dispensed by the ever-present whiskey merchants prompted some of the Ottawas to return to Ohio. On the other hand, some benevolent white residents of Cincinnati gave many of the Ottawas their first outfit of "white man's clothes."[32]

Neither the Baptists nor the government were able to persuade the Ottawas to take immediate possession of their western lands. At the Delaware-Shawnee Agency the Ottawas were advised that housing was unavailable on their new reservation, nor had ground been broken for the commencement of farming. There was no mission and certainly no school. The nearest trading posts for consumer supplies were across the Missouri border, more than a day's journey to the east. And like most other recently arrived emigrants from the Old Northwest, the Ottawas were fearful of physical retaliations from the Pawnees, the Otoes, the Kansas, and the Osages, who understandably resented the arrival of thousands of alien Indians who might attempt to preempt the Arkansas and Smoky valley bison grounds on the west.

A personal visit to the Marais des Cygnes valley by Oquanoxie and seven other Ottawa leaders, in company with Agent Cummins, in February, 1833, only served to confirm those fears. With the unhappy prospect that the entire program for removing Indians to the trans-Missouri West might be aborted, Special Commissioner Henry L. Ellsworth was authorized by Washington authorities to convene an intertribal council at Fort Leavenworth in November for the purpose of securing promises that all acts of hostility and personal revenge would cease between the various tribes. A surface understanding was reached, but the absence of the powerful Osage leadership indicated that the problem was unresolved. Nevertheless, in the summer of 1834, Oquanoxie and approximately seventy Ottawas left for the Marais des Cygnes reserve with $2,000 that Agent Cummins had released from their land sales in Ohio. That fall a delegation of Roche de Boeuf Ottawas visited them, apparently to determine whether it would be safe to bring their families and fellow tribesmen to the new Canaan.[33]

In the intervening time more Ottawa land in Ohio went under the hammer, and as a consequence more Ottawas emigrated to the west. By the treaties of 1807 and 1817 certain Ottawa bands led by Tushquegan, Meskeman, and Waugan had been awarded 24,320 acres of land near the mouth of the Maumee. Comprising much of the modern harbor city of Toledo, these lands appreciated in value with the canal frenzy that gripped northern Ohio in the early 1830s. To would-be town developers and commercial interests it was unthinkable that these lands should remain off the market. Early in 1833 several Ottawa leaders were persuaded to relinquish common ownership in return for 2,160 of the 24,320 acres that had been patented to individual Ottawas. Significantly, of the twelve individuals or families who had received these very valuable patents, eight affixed their signatory X's to the Ottawa treaty of 1833—including the distinguished chief Autokee, who received 320 acres for his efforts. It was bribery at its best. Nearly $30,000 were earmarked for the payment of old debts; the rank and file were to share in the miserly sum of $18,000, according to the Ottawa treaty of 1831; and the nonpatented tribesmen were obliged to evacuate the area within six months.[34]

That the Ottawas stayed longer in Ohio was due mainly to creditors who presented exorbitant claims for debts and threatened violence if these were not paid in full. Frustrated, disillusioned, and virtually dependent on the few government officials who refused to allow any further exploitation, many of these Ottawas fled to northern Michigan or Walpole and Monitoulin islands in Canada, while a lesser number determined to join their brethren in the future Kansas Territory. When informed of this, the ubiquitous McCoy was quick to respond. On February 1, 1837, he reported to the Indian Office in Washington that eighty-one Ottawas were in residence on the Marais des Cygnes, 250 "should be coming," and an additional 6,500 Michigan Ottawas and Chippewas were "supposed to come." For this unconfirmed deluge of humanity, McCoy had plans for a greatly enlarged reservation that would encompass nearly a million acres. Baptist schools and missions operating among all the emigrant tribes would fuel the fires of moral and intellectual improvement, and as in the past the pan-Indian territorial center was to be located nearby— with McCoy, of course, serving as the executive link between the Indians and the government.[35]

Although the fulfillment of McCoy's dream seemed to be at hand, reality dictated otherwise. On October 6, 1837, 170 apprehensive members of the Roche de Boeuf and Wolf Rapids bands arrived at the mouth of the Kansas River aboard the steamer *St. Peters*. On the following day they began the overland journey to the Ottawa reserve in ten crude wagons supplied at four dollars a day by Westport merchant William M. Chick. Less than two years later, in August, 1839, an additional 108 Ottawas arrived at Chouteau's Landing aboard a steamer they had boarded a week earlier at Portsmouth, Ohio. The final leg to the Marais des Cygnes was made by packhorse. Both groups of emigrants experienced hunger, sickness, desertions, and loss of life along the way. The arrival of the 1839 group was especially foreboding for McCoy and the Baptists, for it included chiefs Autokee and Wauseeonoquet (or Wossaonukwut), both of whom were intractable in their opposition to Christian teaching. For his part, McCoy's dream of an Indian state was shattered by War Department opposition and continued congressional inaction. On November 1, 1841, the Baptist Board of Foreign Missions in Boston terminated what it called its "nominal" association with McCoy, while in Indian country interdenominational bickering over missionary subsidies intensified. The final blow came on February 2, 1842, when McCoy was advised by the commissioner of Indian affairs that his services were no longer needed by the government. Shortly thereafter, he moved to Lexington, Kentucky, where his wife had established permanent residence. The education of some 350 Ottawas in the future Franklin County, Kansas, was left to others.[36]

4

Wilderness Entrepreneurs

McCoy's dismissal by both the government and the Baptist Board of Foreign Missions was a serious blow to the establishment of a model school for the emigrant Indians. Like the demise of the movement to organize the Indian Territory politically, these actions were indicative of serious flaws in the removal policy and the inability of public and religious bureaucracies to change the condition of the American Indian. Whatever else McCoy may have been, he was primarily an optimist and social reformer: one who "attacked the system of law and custom by which the American Indians had been kept in bondage from the time of their first contact with white men." He believed that removal was not enough, and that in the absence of effective tools for moral and intellectual improvement, what had happened to the Ottawas in Michigan and Ohio was surely to be repeated in Kansas.[1]

In June, 1842, McCoy made one last effort to realize his dream for Indian education. At a special meeting of the Western Baptist Publication and Sunday School Society in Louisville, Kentucky, he proposed the organization of the American Indian Mission Association, whose primary objectives were the promotion of the spiritual and temporal welfare of the Indians and "the establishment of schools, both male and female, from primary schools to those of the highest order, which the improving conditions of the Indians may at any time require." The association would operate beyond the control of the Baptist Board of Foreign Missions, and it sought a general sanction from the Baptist General Convention. McCoy was appointed principal agent and corresponding secretary of the association, but was again disappointed when in 1844 the Triennial Baptist General Convention denied adoption of the association in favor of allowing individual missionaries to determine where their organizational allegiance lay. The consequence was bitter bickering between missionaries and confusion on the part of the Indians in the field.[2]

One of McCoy's most vitriolic critics was Jotham Meeker, who in 1837 had taken the position as the first resident missionary at the Ottawa Baptist Mission in Kansas. Writing to prominent church officials in the East, Meeker charged:

> During the past ten or eleven years Br. McCoy and Br. J. [Johnston] Lykins, his son-in-law, have lived, not at Shawanoe Mission House, nor in the Indian Territory, but on their own farms, in the state of Missouri. During which time there have been almost constant jams between them and the missionaries residing at some of the stations. They have continued to present themselves before the Indians, Indian Agents and the U.S. Gov. as the Superintendents of the Mission Stations, often assuming to speak and act as if they were sole managers. Often have the missionaries, for taking a course which they consciously [sic] believed to be right, been severely reprimanded by Br. McCoy and frequently has he reported to the Board [of Foreign Missions] in such a way that it became necessary for the person or persons implicated, to give the other side of the story.[3]

Apart from the general complaints concerning McCoy's resolve to dominate the Baptist effort among the Ottawas and other emigrant tribes, Meeker was responding to a very specific charge that had been leveled against him and his fellow missionaries. On March 22, 1842, McCoy's son-in-law had advised Meeker that the Methodists had recently passed resolutions charging the Baptists with having "lowered the Christian standard and having pursued a course calculated to lead to sinful habits . . . by taking in their members while they were under censure for lying, theft, and drunkness." The letter ended with the admonition, "You may conjecture the effect such a statement may have on us in Washington." Whatever the merits of the charges, Meeker in fact is known to have brought wine and brandy onto the Ottawa reservation contrary to federal law, and the Baptists were unsuccessful in obtaining any immediate government support for their mission school. For their part, the Ottawas reported a sense of hopelessness after their 1842 and 1843 annuities were withheld without explanation. The irony of the situation was that it had been McCoy who had officially licensed Meeker "to preach the Gospel of Christ among the Indians" in 1827, that it was McCoy who had offered to share his government income with Meeker until he could become better established as a missionary, and that it was McCoy who had encouraged and applauded Meeker's decision to minister to the Ottawas in 1833. Once in the new Canaan, the Ottawas became almost hopelessly entrapped between McCoy's grandiose plans and Meeker's more mundane strategy for Indian civilization. Opposition to the latter virtually ended with McCoy's death in 1846.[4]

What had attracted McCoy to Meeker was his training as a printer and his apparent skill in learning Indian languages. A native of Hamilton, Ohio, Meeker had learned the printer's trade in Cincinnati. After his conversion to the Baptist faith in 1825, he had accepted McCoy's official certification as a Baptist Indian missionary as prerequisite to taking the position as a missionary-teacher at the Thomas station in Michigan. There and at the Chippewa mission at Sault Sainte Marie, Meeker experimented with a phonetic system of Indian orthography whereby Indian materials were printed with the characters of the English language. The Board of Foreign Missions was so impressed with Meeker's accomplishments that in 1833 it authorized the purchase of a secondhand Seth Adams press, to be delivered to Meeker's custody at the Shawnee Baptist Mission near Westport. Advised of this, McCoy was ecstatic. Now it would be possible to print the Gospel, tracts, books, and an Indian newspaper that could be "circulated throughout the land" from the proposed Indian political center. The press would also be an invaluable tool in the development of the model Indian school.[5]

McCoy's enthusiasm on this point was offset by Meeker's views regarding Indian schools and the proper role of missionaries in the field. He was wholly disinterested in basic social reform and considered government action incidental to the development of a community of "true-believing" native Christians. He was pious, insular, individualistic, nonpromotional, and firm in his conviction that once the central church bureaucracy had agreed to support individual missions, the missionary should be left alone to educate, convert, and watch over expected lapses in moral behavior. In a particularly revealing letter to mission headquarters in 1841, Meeker reported much "backsliding" among the Indians, but was encouraged because the "pagans were dying at a faster rate than the converts . . . and the result, through the blessing of Providence, has been encouraging." Because of his unhappy experiences at Carey and Thomas and his belief that teaching and preaching were best accomplished in native languages, Meeker favored village day schools, as opposed to boarding schools that took the children away from their parents. But, as will be seen, he would accept an Ottawa boarding school if it was prescribed by higher authority or in response to preferences of the Indians themselves.[6]

The formal inauguration of the Ottawa Baptist Mission began on July 18, 1837, when Meeker and his family unloaded their wagons on the north bank of the Marais des Cygnes near present-day Ottawa. As a certified tribal educator, Meeker carried with him the written authority of Commissioner of Indian Affairs Carey Allen Harris, who was an advocate of village schools and the organization of an Indian Territory under the direct supervision of a non-Indian governor. To Harris, Indian schools were to be essentially instruments of social control. They were to enroll only those Indians with enough stature to influence fellow tribesmen in the veracity of American institutions. A small cabin was quickly erected for Meeker's family, and by October a modest "mission house" had been completed. Meeker himself described this structure as little more than a "crude stable." In February, 1838, Meeker returned to the Shawnee Baptist Mission, where he translated and printed four hundred copies of the *Otawa Musenaikun (Ottawa First Book)*, which included basic "Lessons to the Learner" and selections from the Gospel of Luke. Shortly thereafter Joseph Parks (a Shawnee) and James Findley of Jackson County, Missouri, erected a trading store near the Ottawa Mission in anticipation of the regularly scheduled Ottawa annuity payments. The construction of a small schoolhouse was completed in early summer, and on July 9, 1838, Meeker began the long-awaited educational enterprise on the Marais des Cygnes. Surprisingly, at least to Meeker, the tribal leadership insisted that instruction be conducted in English.[7]

While the Ottawas gave Meeker a friendly reception, the majority refused to attend sabbath meetings or any other religious exercises. Of the twenty-six who in 1838 were persuaded to attend school and occasional "services," Meeker was able to convert only Shonguesh, a minor tribal leader. Almost immediately Shonguesh was designated "Principal Chief of the Ottawa Nation" by Meeker, placed on the government payroll with the title of "Native Assistant," and given the responsibility of attempting to convert his wife and parents. In February, 1840, Meeker reported that Shonguesh's wife had been baptized, but that good news was offset by continued "intemperance and other gross vices" and the antimissionary stance of Chief Autokee.

Autokee was greatly distressed by Meeker's conversion

of Shonguesh and his wife. Aged and extremely sick, the
Ottawa traditionalist called a general council of the tribe
on March 13, at which time he severely denounced Meeker
and his efforts to destroy tribal unity. Speaking through
Kom-Chaw because of his own illness, Autokee accused
the Baptist missionary of "doing great mischief by sepa-
rating families and friends, and making confusion all over
the nation." Meeker's only responsibility was to provide
schooling, said Autokee, and since his efforts in this regard
had been unsuccessful, he had no business on the Ottawa
reservation. Meeker was also accused of outright lying
about "the Creator sending Meeker to the Indians." To
this Meeker responded: "The same persons who placed
the Indians here and protected them, also protected me
here. I stated too, that the Creator of the heavens and the
earth had, I thought, sent me here, and that if he had
sent me, he would protect me so long as he wished me to
remain." On the following day Autokee's condition wors-
ened, and on March 16, Meeker was told that, if he did
not leave voluntarily, he would be forcibly expelled "in
two moons." Just before his death on March 18, Autokee
promised that, if he got well, he would pray for the rest
of his life, but to whom he did not say.[8]

Autokee's death and the death of Chief Wauseeonoquet
the previous January removed important obstacles to Meeker's religious work. With the help of Shonguesh, an additional six Ottawas were baptized on March 29. A gristmill
was put into operation in the spring of 1841, and agricultural activity increased. The devastating flood of 1844,
which destroyed most of the Ottawas' homes and nearly
all their crops, and the tragic drowning of Shonguesh in
June, 1845 (while he was swimming the Marais des Cygnes
en route to a prayer meeting) did little to dampen the spirit
of the young but growing Ottawa Baptist congregation. In
1847 there were sixty-five members, a new log mission
costing $500 had been erected out of reach of flood waters,
and Meeker's success as a frontier missionary was becoming the talk of the Indian country. His educational efforts,

however, were anything but spectacular. From his entire tribe less than a dozen children could be persuaded to attend the Shawnee Manual School.[9]

In a move that Meeker surely considered a mixed blessing, pressure for the establishment of an Ottawa boarding school came from the government. On January 27, 1848, the Saint Louis Indian superintendent Thomas H. Harvey, met with the Ottawas at their reservation. As reported by Meeker, Harvey was impressed with the Ottawas' "piety" and well-tended fields. His main object, however, was to induce the tribe to put forth a financial effort among themselves to establish a boarding school. Noting that an $800 sum only recently paid out of the Civilization Fund for a Potawatomi Catholic school was no longer needed, Harvey promised that, if the Ottawas committed some of their own money, he would write the War Department and request that the $800 be divided between a Wea and an Ottawa boarding school. In response, the Ottawas said they supported the plan for a boarding school, but because of trader debts still unpaid under the treaty of 1833, they could commit no more than $150 the first year. To his superiors Meeker wrote: "From my letter of Jan 15 [1848] you without doubt infer that I am opposed to have a [boarding] school established here. Mrs. Meeker and I have been thinking over the whole matter and feel that we are perhaps opposing the designs of Providence, and wish to yield to the superior judgement of the Ex. Committee." In Boston the board applauded Harvey's recommendation, but refused to make any money available. If the Ottawas were to have a school, they or the government (or both) would have to assume the financial responsibility. The Baptists would provide the personnel.[10]

Meeker continued to send mostly positive reports regarding the progress of the Ottawas. At the same time he was being pressured by the government and the church to have the Indians commit more of their resources for the school. "Worldly-mindedness" was the phrase that Meeker typically used in describing life on the Marais des

Cygnes, but a better word might have been "materialistic."
The Ottawas had as their model the white settlers who
were beginning to invade the area. In July, 1849, Meeker
reported, "The missionary deplores the existence in the
church of worldly-mindedness and spiritual sloth to a greater extent than in former years." Later that year he wrote,
"They are becoming every year more and more civilized,
and are endeavoring to imitate the whites. . . . A spirit
of worldly-mindedness seems to be increasing." Three years
later he reported, "There is general indifference to spiritual things among them, which is difficult to overcome;
but in other respects their condition and tendencies leave
little to be desired."[11]

Sectional tension, economic pressure in favor of con-
structing a transcontinental railroad west of Missouri, and
the movement to organize the Kansas-Nebraska Territory
in the early 1850s placed enormous pressure on Meeker,
though it is doubtful that he perceived the implications for
his work among the Ottawas. Until instructed otherwise,
he was content to report the conversion of nearly half
the tribe, including six official "Cathechists, Exhorters, or
Aids in the Dissemination of the Gospel," or such mundane activities as setting out "150 cabbage plants." Four
hundred acres were under native cultivation, and more
than a hundred cattle and two hundred hogs were providing a worthy complement to the $2,600 issued by the
government each year. A temperance society had been
organized, an "anti-running-in-debt" law had been passed,
and fighting, stealing, drinking, swearing, and conjugal
infidelity were at a minimum. In short, the Christian faction seemed to be prevailing over paganism.[12]

Brusquely, in the summer of 1853, this seemingly idyllic
situation was disrupted. From the Baptist hierarchy came
information that a treaty was pending with the Ottawas,
and that Meeker should accept as prudently as possible
any offer extended to him to become an official member
of the tribe. The precedent certainly was there, for at that
time there were at least three "European or white heads

of families," as well as twenty-five mixed-blood children, recognized as tribal members.

Word had gotten around that Indian Commissioner George Manypenny was on his way to the Indian country and that he intended to ascertain the Ottawas' disposition regarding a "proposed purchase." Meeker dutifully submitted a map to the commissioner drawn by an unidentified Indian hunter, which purportedly documented the topographical attractiveness of building the Pacific Railroad across the lands of the Peorias, Ottawas, and Sacs and Foxes. Meeker emphasized that he was not attempting to pressure the Ottawas, who gave every indication that they were uninterested in selling their reservation; but he admitted, "It is true, I have my preferences and on suitable occasions I express them to our Agent [Burton A. James] and other friends—but shall endeavor, in no way, to interfere with the plans of the government."

A year later Meeker reported that the Ottawas were virtually surrounded by white squatters, many of whom were running whiskey shops on the very boundaries of the Ottawa reservation. Meeker advised that the Ottawas were "much agitated" about their lands and adamant in their belief that their condition would not be improved by moving to any other place. By then Meeker's physical condition was deteriorating rapidly, and on January 12, 1855, he died. Grief-stricken, his widow wrote:

As to the poor forsaken Indians I know not what to say. They feel that they have lost a true friend, and will never find another. In addition to this they are in a suffering condition. On account of the great failure of the crops last season they are left without anything to eat. Some of them are now living on roots. I fear they will die of hunger. Provisions are very high here. The white people who are settling around us are some of the worst in the world, and are standing ready to injure the Indians in every possible way in their power. This little Church is smitten. The tender benches are surrounded by enemies.[13]

With the death of Meeker the education of the Ottawas came under the guidance of more aggressive men—men who saw in the political and economic development of the Kansas-Nebraska Territory a means whereby schools, land, natural resources, and a strategic location could be exploited for personal advantage. These wilderness entrepreneurs mixed piety with ambition, for they saw no essential conflict between material gain and God's calling to them to instruct the less wise in the workings of civilization. If a conflict developed between the two, they were ill prepared to sacrifice personal aggrandizement for higher calling, mostly for the reason that they viewed their actions as exemplary. Clearly they considered that righteousness was on their side. They would literally demand the cooperation of the Indians and the assistance of the government in pursuit of "progress," without seriously questioning or reflecting on the moral questions involved. The choice was theirs, not the Ottawas. As Bernard Sheehan has stated, "If the Indian could not be introduced into civilization through the formal procedures of presentation and conversion, then he would have to be slipped in through adroit manipulation."[14]

Railroad talk filled the air in frontier Kansas, but on the Ottawa reserve the government's Civilization Fund attracted more immediate attention. Strapped for funds for his struggling mission, in a manner reminiscent of the Carey and Thomas missions in Michigan, Meeker had complained that the Catholics were receiving too much of the abundant Potawatomi civilization fund in Kansas. By the treaty of 1837 the Potawatomis had been awarded a large reservation immediately south and east of the Ottawas', and it was difficult for the Baptists to observe what they called "popery" underwritten so close at hand. Interdenominational bickering and competition for government money, of course, were not unique to Kansas, but they had a particular significance there, because they soon provided the avenue whereby John Tecumseh (Tauy) Jones became involved and eventually dominant in the increasingly complex educational affairs of the Ottawas.[15]

By any kind of character appraisal, Jones was a fascinating and controversial individual. A mixed-blood, he had a shrewd awareness of what Indian acculturation and intertribal politics might mean in the economic development of the frontier. He mixed personal piety, individual gain, and government subsidy with impunity, and he certainly perceived the importance of religious fervor in the developing educational enterprise among the Ottawas.

Born in Canada in 1808 to an English father and Chippewa mother, Jones had lived as a youth with a sister on Mackinac Island and later with a certain Captain Conner in Detroit. After Conner's death in 1825, Jones was baptized by McCoy at Carey, where he studied languages and regained a considerable fluency in Chippewa and Potawatomi. His apparent talent for learning in general so impressed his mentors that they sent him to various eastern schools, including Columbia College (now George Washington University) in Washington, D.C., and Madison Seminary (now Colgate University) in New York state. Throughout that period Jones impressed the Baptists with his potential as a teacher, though one did complain that he needed "a little more stability." In any case, the Madison faculty requested that "owing to failing health" he withdraw from his studies, after which he served for a short while as a government interpreter at the Sault Sainte Marie Indian Agency. Following that he took a position as "native teacher" at Col. Richard M. Johnson's Choctaw Academy in the bluestem country of Kentucky, but as in the past he continued to have personal problems and difficulties with the school's administrators.

In 1836, on learning that the Indiana Potawatomis had agreed to remove to the Indian country west of Missouri, Jones determined that his destiny lay in more virgin country. Securing a formal Potawatomi adoption for himself and his non-Indian wife, he journeyed to the new Potawatomi reservation in Kansas's present-day Miami County. There he staked a claim to a comfortable farm site and as-

sociated himself with Rev. John G. Pratt's nearby Stockbridge (Baptist) Indian school, while his wife taught a few
Potawatomis under government contract. Although he was
suspended from the local Baptist congregation for backsliding, he was later reinstated as a member. He awaited
what he repeatedly described as "the guiding hand of Providence."[16]

The pressure of white encroachment on the Missouri
border forced the Potawatomis to relinquish their lands
on the eastern edge of the Indian country, and in 1847
they signed a new treaty, which provided them with a new
tract about 100 miles to the northwest in the lower Kansas
River valley. Jones apparently was concerned that this
arrangement might jeopardize the fee-simple title by which
he hoped one day to protect his personal stake in the now-
ceded Potawatomi reserve. He advised Meeker that for
the time being nothing could be done to improve the lot
of the Potawatomis. Adding to Jones's problems was criti-
cism coming from Baptist headquarters of his ability as a
Potawatomi interpreter and the unreliable translations he
was providing for Meeker's Indian Bible Society publica-
tions. Jones maintained that the well-being of his family
required that he attend more closely to his own business
affairs, but in fact, the Potawatomi leadership had raised
serious doubts about Jones's character when in 1845 it was
announced that he was to be their "assistant missionary"
at $125 per annum. In 1848 their doubts turned into angry
objections when Jones made an abortive attempt, "as recommended by all the Pot. traders, their Agent, and Superintendent in St. Louis," to draw $1,000 from their 1847
treaty fund for the value of his recently acquired farm.

Nevertheless, Meeker continued to support Jones. He
had presided over Jones's second marriage to Rachel Little-
ton (a Stockbridge Indian) at the Ottawa Mission in 1840,
and following Rachel's untimely death in 1844, had conducted Jones's third marriage to Jane Kelly (a non-Indian
teacher at Stockbridge) the following spring. He repeatedly
described Jones as a "good worker" and seemed to be es-

pecially impressed with the piety and dedication of his successive wives. Meeker did admit to his Baptist superiors that "the Catholics had brought forward a difficulty in which Jones had become embroiled some twelve or fourteen years ago at Col. R. M. Johnson's Academy," and that they had "induced the Inds. to fear that Col. Johnson will yet make a [financial] haul on the Potawatomi Nation for heavy damages on Jones' account." Nevertheless, he emphasized: "My private opinion is *now,* that this effort of the Jesuits will not injure his [Jones'] usefulness. . . . He is a useful brother—he embraces many opportunities to do good . . . [and] expects to remain on his farm this winter, and try to watch the leading of Providence."[17]

Jones was more realistic. While Meeker continued to promote him as the ideal man for the Potawatomi assignment, Jones directed his attention toward the Ottawas. Late in 1847, while he occupied a farm valued at $1,000 on the Ottawa reservation, he persuaded the Ottawas to welcome him and his bride into the circle of tribal membership and brought pressure on Meeker and other Baptist leaders to establish a boarding school. In this he was encouraged because what was loosely called the "Ottawa District Mission School" was then under fire. This village-type school had been operated under Meeker's direction by Elizabeth S. Morse. Attendance had steadily declined since its organization in the summer of 1847, and by January, 1848, enrollment was down to four or five students per month. The Ottawas saw no good reason to fund such an obviously unpopular endeavor, and when Miss Morse took a position at the Delaware Baptist Mission later that year, the school was closed. While continuing to support the concept of Indian schools in general, the ever-cautious Meeker noted that, "because the calls were heavy and so often repeated for funds to support schools and the preaching of the gospel throughout the larger heathen nations of the earth," it was premature to think of any large educational expenditures at Ottawa at that time. Jones's patience was exhausted, and in October he bluntly informed Meeker that he could wait no longer. Destiny, he said, was pointing in a different direction and the Ottawas had invited him to serve "as their only [government] trader." It was a move bordering on the prophetic, for by then the Baptist Board in Boston had advised Meeker, "You may say to the Ottawas that there is reason to hope for a Boarding School, though not just now, and the Committee would appoint Br. and Sr. Jones if anyone to take charge."[18]

While Jones continued to pressure the Indian Office in Washington for certification of his land claim against his late Potawatomi brethren, the Ottawas contracted financial obligations at his store to the total amount of their next annuity. And at his urging, they reaffirmed their desire "to have a respectful school one day." Meeker was even more cooperative. In terms clearly indicative of his preference for religious as opposed to secular employment, the aging Baptist missionary reported to Superintendent Thomas Harvey in Saint Louis that Jones and his wife were out of work and "patiently awaiting divine guidance." As for the faculty of the much-discussed boarding school, Meeker emphasized that "no persons anywhere would be more cordially received by the Ottawas than they." Harvey, however, insisted that the government might be more interested in a financial commitment if the Baptists would match their words of optimism with a donation from their own coffers. It was indeed a frustrating situation for Jones.[19]

New hope for Jones and his supporters sprang from the formal organization of the Kansas-Nebraska Territory in the spring of 1854. With a horde of speculators poised on the western border of Missouri awaiting the signal from the Franklin Pierce administration to preempt the most attractive lands in Kansas, Jones and the Baptists could take comfort in their dominant location on the Ottawa reserve—a strategic position from which to guide the development of a virgin territory. It mattered little that the Ottawas manifested "little special religious interests." Many had become nominal Baptists; most lived on fairly comfortable farms; and compared to the nearby Sacs and Foxes, who in candor admitted their "tremendous horror of missionaries," the Ottawas seemed more than ready for the kind of treaty making that might make an educational enterprise profitable for all.[20]

"In regard to the settlement of this country and the effect it may have on missions," advised the Reverend John G. Pratt to Meeker in 1853, "nothing can be conjectured until something is known as to the character of the treaties." Pratt's uncertainty was well founded, for the Ottawas proved more obstinate than Jones and Meeker had anticipated. With their experiences in Ohio and Michigan still fresh in their memories, the Ottawas were not wholly naive regarding frontier politics and the possible implications of the Kansas-Nebraska Act. In late December, 1853, Meeker reported to Rev. S. Peck that the Ottawas would sell none of their lands and that a treaty along those lines was simply "out of the question." Rather their plan was to divide their lands equally among themselves, ask President Pierce for patents in fee simple, and become citizens of the United States. Nothing was said about education. Indeed, as late as July, 1859, Agent Perry Fuller reported, "There seems to be a great lack of interest among them on the subject of education."[21]

Jones, however, was not to be denied. He was after all an official member of the tribe, the licensed Ottawa trader-creditor, a man of stature in the local Baptist establishment and in a position to exert considerable influence on those members of the tribal council who, following passage of the Kansas-Nebraska Bill, began to appreciate the speculative character of frontier economic development on the model of Jones. Not surprisingly then, the Ottawas, with the encouragement of their leaders, began to modify their position regarding a treaty. In November, 1854, they informed Commissioner George Manypenny of their desire to have their annuities commuted for the aggregate sum of $52,000 and to sell a strip of reservation land two miles wide for the modest sum of $1.00 per acre. In August, 1855, they insisted the deal must go through before the next session of Congress. In April, 1856, they reported that "in open council" the tribe had agreed to send Kom-Chaw, Shaw-Pom-Da (Pahtee), and John T. Jones to Washington to expedite a treaty incorporating these considerations.[22]

During those turbulent years the pro- and antislavery interests were competing, sometimes violently, sometimes subtly, for the economic and political domination of Kansas Territory. It was not at all difficult for a man of Jones's caliber to become involved in the thick of the struggle. The combination dwelling, hotel, and Indian trading post that he had erected on Ottawa land about four miles northeast of present-day Ottawa, Kansas, became a popular stopping place for Free-Soil partisans traveling from Lawrence to Fort Scott. As such, his facility was a prime target for proslavery forces who were angered by his apparent sympathy with the radical abolitionism of John Brown. Consequently, in August, 1856, the infamous Border Ruffians allegedly burned Jones's establishment to the ground, though there is evidence that at least some of the debt-ridden Ottawas who resented Jones's increasing power in the tribal council had equal justification for this act of violence. In any case, the incident placed Jones in an economic situation no less frustrating than that which he had only recently experienced on the ceded Potawatomi reserve. The difference was that his loss at the hands of a more accessible enemy provided him with a much better opportunity to further his own interests. He pressed a claim against the federal government for the loss of his buildings, gold, and personal property, which a sympathetic government official valued at $8,400. He had been "badly treated," said Sac and Fox Agent Francis Tymony, in fact so badly treated that four years later Indian Commissioner A. B. Greenwood conceded that, given the turbulent state of affairs in Kansas at that time, the government should pay the claim without even conducting an investigation. Clearly Jones was a man of influence and one to be reckoned with.[23]

From Jones's perspective, a carefully structured treaty

was mandatory—one that would satisfy his immediate needs while placating the various tribal interests. With chiefs Kom-Chaw and Shaw-Pom-Da (Pahtee) and tribal delegate Thomas Wolf, Jones journeyed to Washington early in the summer of 1857. There they met with Indian Commissioner James Denver and worked out a settlement that was personally advantageous to them. As proposed, the 74,000-acre reservation was to be disposed of in the following manner:

- Two sections (1,280 acres) were to be reserved for a common school district under Kansas territorial law.
- Twenty acres were to be reserved for the Baptist Church, its mission buildings, and burial ground.
- A townsite of 640 acres was to be reserved and subdivided into equal lots corresponding to the number of Ottawa families and adult unmarried males, and the lots were to be granted to those groups or individuals in fee simple.
- The two daughters of Jotham Meeker were each to be given 320 acres.
- Chiefs Kom-Chaw and Shaw-Pom-Da and delegate John T. Jones were each scheduled to receive 320 acres; delegate Thomas Wolf was to receive 160 acres.
- The remaining lands were to be divided by a "Distribution Commission" to all tribal members, as best as possible to include improvements already made.

In addition, all previous annuities, school funds, and services provided by the government were to be voided in favor of a lump-sum settlement of $66,000, which was to be divided equally among the tribal membership. A $6,690.80 trust fund based on the treaty of 1831 was to be paid and similarly distributed. Any land remaining was to be sold for the benefit of the tribe, and the government was to investigate all depredations committed by whites against Ottawa individuals. Over and above the general tribal distribution, Kom-Chaw, Shaw-Pom-Da (Pahtee), and Jones were each to receive $1,000 in cash, while Wolf's personal award was half that amount. Finally, Jones's loss of

August 29, 1856, was to be adjusted by the commissioner
of Indian affairs and promptly paid by the government.
A boarding school was not even mentioned.[24]
The proposed settlement was clearly divisive. Rev. E.
Willard, who had temporarily replaced Meeker at the Baptist mission, reported in the summer of 1858:

> The Ottawas sent their first deputation to Washington two
> years ago next month; since then, they have been idle, running
> into debt in the hope of paying off when they become citizens. The outsiders no longer like to trust them, and at this
> moment they are straitened for food. If the [1857] treaty is
> not finally ratified, and soon too, it is difficult to imagine what
> they will do. . . . You will also take into account that Br.
> Jones has been absent five months of every ten, or nearly so,
> since he arrived, and there is no other interpreter. . . . Circumstances have not been favorable to spiritual progress. In
> addition, there are too many whiskey-sellers on the outside;
> so that all things considered, the wonder is that they hold on
> at all.[25]

Malcolm White, the Ottawa agent, complained that in violation of federal trade and intercourse acts, his wards were
dividing the reservation into individual claims, renting the
most valuable plots to white squatters, and selling timber
and rails for individual profit, Jones and the tribal council
engaged the services of A. G. Sheldon, former government
surveyor from Lawrence, to survey the reservation "in anticipation of the treaty." The survey was completed in
March, 1859, over the objections of the United States Indian Office, which by that time had repudiated the 1857
treaty. Undaunted, Jones and his followers came back with
a new proposal the following November: of the total of
74,000 acres, 160 acres were to be given to each member
of the tribe; forty acres were reserved for a church; 320
acres for a school; 320 acres would be granted to Reverend
Meeker's daughters; and 2,560 acres would be placed in
the hands of Chief Kom-Chaw for what was vaguely termed
"general tribal welfare." Unallotted land would be sold to

white settlers at not less than $1.25 per acre. From those sales $40,000 would be invested for the support of the industrial school over a twenty-five year period. After individual allotments had been selected, the Ottawas would have to wait a minimum of five years to become United States citizens. Finally, Jones was to receive 960 acres above his tribal allotment, as well as a cash payment of $1,000 for certain undesignated "services."[26]

On the surface, this second "Denver Treaty" (named for Indian Commissioner James Denver) appeared to enjoy smooth sailing, particularly with the rudder in the hands of "Ottawa Jones" (as the new Ottawa leader was now called). Yet almost immediately some of the more traditionalist members of the tribe began to ask embarrassing questions. Why was Jones, only recently adopted by the tribe, promised fully five times as much as the rank and file? What was the reason for the $1,000 payment? Had this man, who claimed Christian piety, been completely honest in his credit dealings with the tribe as a whole? In December, 1859, Sac and Fox Agent Perry Fuller admitted that "all the worry is about Jones and his land." Even the tribal council was beginning to divide, with one faction holding out for only 640 acres for Jones and only $480 in cash. By May, 1860, matters had gone from bad to worse. "The Ottawas will not make a treaty at St. Louis or St. Joseph [Missouri] but insist on coming directly to Washington," reported Fuller; and worse, Jones was losing his influence with the younger members of the tribe. Clearly, the embattled Baptist Indian of many faces was in need of assistance—which from his perspective, Providence was quick to provide.[27]

5

The Grand Design

SUPPORT for the beleaguered Jones came in the person of Clinton Carter Hutchinson, better known as "C.C." to his friends and close associates. A true believer in unrestrained economic enterprise and straightforward frontierstyle religion, Hutchinson hailed from the abolitionist stronghold of Vermont. Following a brief, abortive experience as a Chicago land speculator, Hutchinson came to Kansas Territory in 1856, where he served as an agent for the American Baptist Home Mission Society and occasionally preached fire and brimstone from a pulpit in the frontier village of Topeka. By the summer of 1857 he had taken a squatter claim in Franklin County, was recognized as a prominent officer in the newly created Kansas State Agricultural Society, and like his close friend Tauy Jones, was persuaded that the Marais des Cygnes valley was the land of promise. The only problem was the Indians.[1]

With Jones serving as his mentor, it was not difficult for Hutchinson to perceive how he might play an important role in the unfolding dispensation. A massive turnover in Indian Office personnel was assured by the election of Lincoln in 1860, and the Sac and Fox Agency, which then had jurisdiction over the Ottawas, would shortly become vacant. Who was better qualified to look after the educational needs of a "savage" but peaceful people than a

Baptist mission agent with good political connections and some experience in land speculation? Appraising the situation carefully, Jones and Hutchinson exerted pressure on Indian Commissioner William Dole, and on April 3, 1861, Hutchinson received his appointment as Sac and Fox agent. From the start Hutchinson seems to have understood the importance of conducting the fiscal affairs of his office in a manner calculated to obstruct, or at least to complicate, any future accounting that might be required. Writing to Central Superintendent H. B. Branch on September 10, 1861, Hutchinson requested that the annuities for his agency be issued in low-denomination treasury drafts. He added that it would be a "material accommodation to the business public in Kansas" if he could receive all other public funds in the form of specie. To this Branch was surprisingly agreeable, and within a short time a shipment of $18,900 worth of coin was delivered to Hutchinson in Leavenworth, at a cost of $70 freight. Clearly, the Indian Office at the superintendency level had great confidence in C.C. and, in fact, was encouraging him to take financial liberties that were not in the best interests of his Indian wards.

Less than a year later, when it became apparent that the Ottawa educational enterprise would be greatly enhanced by the creation of a separate Ottawa Indian Agency, Hutchinson was appointed as agent—even though he had been dismissed from his Sac and Fox post for fraud and had been characterized by one government official as "unfit" for the Indian service. It mattered little that three Sac and Fox chiefs accused him of misusing $2,000 that they had been encouraged to borrow from Thomas Carney, prominent Leavenworth Indian and War Department contractor and political broker in Kansas, or that Agent Hutchinson cursed and abused them on repeated occasions, or that he had neglected them in favor of the Ottawas. Following Tauy Jones's timely advice to authorities in Washington that "a combination of proslavery men and a drunken Sac and Fox halfblood" were attempting falsely to represent Hutchinson, Superintendent Branch testified that Hutchinson enjoyed a "perfect knowledge of the wants and necessities of the Ottawas and from his well-known efficiency as an agent I cheerfully join with him and his numerous friends on recommending him for the position."[2]

The government's facile acquiescence obviously was pleasing to Jones, but good fortune in the developing plan for an Indian university seemed all the more assured with the emergence of yet another Baptist notable in the affairs of the Ottawas. The Reverend Isaac S. Kalloch was "a tall, slim-waisted, red-headed, pink-whiskered" preacher from Boston. He soon was characterized by some Kansans as the "Sorrell Stallion of the Marais des Cygnes." Apparently this uncryptic appellation was no mere speculation, for before his arrival in Kansas, Kalloch had been involved in some moral indiscretions that had compromised his effectiveness as a man of the cloth. The most notable affair was allegedly with a certain Mrs. J. F. Steen (née Laura Flye), one of Isaac's childhood sweethearts, whom he was said to have wooed in an East Cambridge, Massachusetts, hotel while Mrs. Kalloch was ill in nearby Boston. While the details of the incident remain sketchy, it did lead, in 1857, to one of the most celebrated adultery trials in antebellum New England. The performance of defense attorney Richard Henry Dana was sufficient to convince the jury that the charismatic pastor of Boston's famous Tremont (Baptist) Temple was guilty of no specific legal infraction, but in the wake of the trial, public opinion augured against him to such a degree that Kalloch was unable to carry on his pastoral duties effectively. So he had come to Kansas to repair his career.[3]

Kalloch first arrived in 1857, under the auspices of Eli Thayer's New England Emigrant Aid Society, and a second time in 1860, as a field representative for the American Baptist Home Mission Society. His outside interests were many, including raising blooded cattle, horse trading, horse racing, and lecturing on the evils of slavery in Kansas. He helped found Bluemont Central College (forerunner of the present Kansas State University) by serving as a fund raiser, was admitted to the Kansas bar, formed a law partnership with Judge John T. Pendery (who had administered his bar examination), and dabbled briefly in squatter and Indian land claims. One local editor claimed that, what with his "insatiable desires for money, whiskey and women," Kansas was simply too confining for Kalloch. Perhaps it was, but a more plausible explanation for his departure was the disastrous drought of 1859 and 1860 and the consequent recession, which plagued speculators in frontier Kansas. In any case, Kalloch returned east a few months later to become pastor of the fashionable Laight Street Baptist Church in New York City. Despite reports that he consumed indecent quantities of whiskey and continued to visit the local "houses of ill-fame," Kalloch's New York parishioners were more than pleased with his performance, for as a fund raiser and public speaker he was absolutely superb.

Why then did Kalloch return to Kansas a third time in 1864? Certainly his amorous reputation had preceded him, as one Kansas editor emphasized in a warning from Job 40:16-17 to young women who had been maneuvered west by agents of the New England Emigrant Aid Society and might encounter Kalloch: "Lo, now, his strength is in his loins, and his force is in the naval of his belly. He moveth his tail like a cedar; the sinews of his stones are wrapped together." Kalloch himself simply stated that the Lord was leading the way, but more temporal guidance had come from C. C. Hutchinson, who on February 5, 1864, wrote Rev. John G. Pratt: "Our college and *colony* [emphasis added] enterprise look very favorable and I have great faith in it. I very much want Bro. K. [Kalloch] to *commence* with us. If he goes many other No. 1 men will go, who will not go without him and his name will do much for us." Reports also were circulating that alliances previously forged by Jones and Hutchinson with Kansas Governor Charles Robinson, Senators James Lane and Samuel Pomeroy, and other political notables in Kansas were beginning to pay dividends. More important, through the Baptist hierarchy in the East the Reverend Isaac Kalloch had obtained a Western "preferment which one day would be invaluable."[4]

"Invaluable" was putting it mildly, as Jones surely must have known for some time. He was in need of assistance because, while serving as the principal advocate of Ottawa education in 1859, he had overplayed his hand. He had been rebuked for attempting to speculate in Potawatomi land. Moreover, Jones's failure to profit personally at the hands of the Potawatomis was matched by the Baptists' failure to commit $100,000 in support of general tribal education, as Hutchinson and Kalloch had promised certain Ottawa chiefs that same year.

Under the circumstances lesser men might have been discouraged, but these were no ordinary men. They knew what they wanted; they believed that providence and progress worked hand in hand; and in the name of enterprise they were prepared to take risks. Acres upon acres of prime prairie land lay unproductive, timber was in bountiful supply, potential town lots seemed to be begging to appreciate in value, ribbons of rail iron were stretching toward the territory, and the Ottawas meanwhile remained committed to moral improvement. What remained was to secure legal sanctions from both the tribe and the government that all would profit from a new arrangement. Precisely who had assumed the role of master architect by 1860 is difficult to determine, but this much is certain: Ottawa Jones, the adopted Indian; Hutchinson, soon to be the government agent; and Kalloch, the evangelical educator, constituted a formidable trinity who would be difficult to contain. With the assistance of such other territorial dignitaries as S. B. Prentiss, Jesse Cinell, R. C. Brant, Benjamin Luce, J. J. Emory, E. Allward, John Drew, Augustus Isboll, L. A. Alderson, W. O. Thomas, J. B. Maynard, Wm. J. Kermott, and Wm. H. Russell, a charter of incorporation for the "Roger Williams University" was obtained from the territorial legislature in the spring of 1860.

The corporate body empowered was a group of "leading Baptists of Kansas" with tax-exempt authority to operate a university at an undesignated place in Kansas Territory, and to offer degrees in the liberal arts, sciences, medicine, law, and theology.

According to one twentieth-century Ottawa University source, the Reverend L. A. Alderson, at a Baptist convention in Atchison later that year, suggested to Tauy Jones that, "since the [Ottawa] Indians have the land which might be converted into money, and since the whites have the ability to carry forward an educational program," Roger Williams University should be located on the Ottawa reserve. A Committee of Roger Williams University was duly organized in December, 1860, which "by invitation of the Ottawas in full council" secured a written statement (branded fraudulent by federal investigators in 1872) that the tribe would give the Baptists, for the purpose of boarding, clothing, and educating fifty of their children for the next thirty years, 20,000 acres of "average" reservation land. In return the trustees of the university were to spend $10,000 on buildings. In 1865 the university was renamed Ottawa University to discourage impressions that the government was aiding a denominational school.

A land-development corporation was to be formed under the leadership of Hutchinson and Kalloch. Outside money for sustaining the project would be attracted from eastern investors, white settlers would be allowed to buy the acreage that remained after each Ottawa Indian had selected his own 160-acre plot, a townsite would be developed, and whatever details remained to be considered the Ottawa tribe would leave to the government. Writing to Indian Commissioner A. B. Greenwood with aggressive confidence, Kalloch and Jones explained: "Some of the most responsible men in Boston as well as Kansas [are] in on this [and] will get 40-50,000 acres of unoccupied land into immediate settlement and educate the whole tribe for thirty years and relieve government from further expenses with them."5

Probably because he was a lame-duck Indian commissioner, Greenwood took no action. Jones and Kalloch had enlisted the support of Ottawa councilman William Hurr for the 1860 proposal, but with the Indian Department undergoing a major realignment following a presidential election, additional tribal support was deemed desirable. Land was the bait, and with the promise of 320 acres each for their cooperation, Pem-ach-wung and James Wind joined forces with the Baptists. To them it apparently mattered little that intratribal factionalism was further encouraged, or that Hutchinson's malpractices as Sac and Fox agent were leading at that very time to his dismissal from that post. Fulfillment was at hand. In May, 1862, Hutchinson advised Indian Commissioner William Dole that, with "nearly every member of the tribe consenting," the Ottawas had agreed to send Pem-ach-wung, Hurr, Jones, and Wind to Washington to work out the details. The negotiations proceeded on schedule, and the treaty that was proclaimed on July 28, 1862, guaranteed virtually everything that the Baptists had hoped for.[6]

For the most part the treaty appeared uncontroversial. Following an introductory observation that the tribe was "sufficiently advanced in civilization" to join white society —an observation that was to cause enormous legal problems in the future—it was agreed that each Ottawa family head would receive 160 acres, and all others eighty acres, if they agreed to renounce tribal affiliation within five years and become citizens of the United States. A small annuity was promised; tribal debts were to be paid out of future tribal income; a plot of land was set aside for an Ottawa Baptist Church; Reverend Meeker's children were to receive eighty acres each; and a portion of the reservation totaling approximately 30,000 acres was to be sold to "industrious whites" at a price of not less than $1.25 per acre. In the future the lands of this last class were usually designated as "trust lands." Individual Ottawa farmsteads were to be "adjoining, and in as regular and compact form as possible"; significantly for Tauy Jones and his retinue, five sections were set apart for the tribal chief and his councilmen as just compensation for their services. The division of this land was finally accomplished in December, 1863. Jones took 960 acres; Pem-ach-wung, Hurr, and Wind received 320 acres each; and several smaller plots of land went to less distinguished leaders, whose support for the treaty was thereby recognized. Councilman John Wilson also received 320 acres, which, it turned out, was not enough to placate his increasing suspicion regarding the justice of the settlement.[7]

Lengthy Article Six was anything but orthodox, and it constituted the nucleus of the treaty. It was in fact the mechanism that implemented the grand design for dispossessing the Ottawas. Deeming the occasion a "favorable opportunity" to provide for the education of their posterity, the Ottawas were urged to accept the following arrangements:

— Twenty thousand acres of "average lands" were to be set aside to endow a school "for the benefit of the Ottawas."

— An additional section of land was to be set apart for the school building itself and related appurtenances.

— For the construction of the building and other "improvements," five thousand of the twenty thousand acres were to be sold under the supervision of a board of trustees comprised of Jones, Wind, Hurr, and King (who were all identified as bona fide Ottawa Indians), and John G. Pratt and two other white citizens of Kansas to be designated by the tribe.

The sale of the residue fifteen thousand acres of school lands was also to be supervised by this board, which could transact no formal business unless at least two of the white trustees were present. Money received from the sale of this residue school land was to be "loaned upon good real estate security, to be improved as farms in the country of the reservation . . . and the interest only [was] to be applied to the support of the school, so that the principal [would never] be diminished." So that the Ottawas might derive the best advantage from the school, the pupils were to be instructed in "industrial pursuits . . . as well as in such branches of learning as the means of the institution and their capacity [would] permit." Finally, it was stipulated that the children of the Ottawas and their descendants, no matter where they might emigrate, were to have the right to enter the school "and enjoy all the privileges thereof, the same as though they had remained upon the lands by this treaty allotted."[8]

Not unexpectedly, the two white citizens elected to the all-important University Board of Trustees were Clinton C. Hutchinson and Isaac S. Kalloch. Kalloch in fact, was designated president of the board after James Wind dutifully offered to resign in 1864. In addition, John W. Young—Hutchinson's father-in-law—purchased on August 20, 1862, the entire 5,000 acres of University development land at the minimum price of $1.25. Providence, it appeared, was not only kind but generous as well.[9]

Meanwhile, in the fall of 1862, Hutchinson's appointment as Sac and Fox agent was terminated. Although there were a variety of reasons, including his chronic absence from his agency headquarters, his abuseful and neglectful treatment of his wards, and his involvement in questionable land deals, the immediate cause was Hutchinson's having forced the Sacs and Foxes, without the required approval of his government superiors, to borrow $2,000 from future Kansas Governor Thomas Carney to go to Washington. The purpose of the journey was not clear at the time, but in retrospect, it was to line Hutchinson's own pockets. Secretary of the Interior John P. Usher was enraged, charging that even if Hutchinson could explain how the money had been used, which he could not, he "was not a proper person to be an Indian agent." "I was the more prompted to ask for his removal," emphasized Usher, "because the money for which he has rendered no account whatsoever was at least twice the amount of the Indians' proper expenses to this city." Usher's position was reasonable, and at this point Hutchinson's career with the Indian

Office should have been permanently abrogated and carefully investigated. Certainly nothing in the files of the Interior Department suggests even the remotest possibility that he could have been exonerated in a judicial hearing. But Usher was a busy man, and apparently he was unable to perceive the objectives of the complex scheme that was unfolding in Kansas.

To Commissioner Dole, Hutchinson explained that the secretary was simply unable to appreciate his (Hutchinson's) position in proper context and that Usher had deployed "summary methods" in his recent dismissal. Above all, it was absolutely essential that he, as the Ottawas' "special agent," should direct the tribe in their sincere efforts to carry out to the letter the enterprise contemplated in their recent treaty with the United States. He was the only official capable of contending with the unprincipled and land-hungry whites surrounding the Ottawa reserve, and he had kept his long-range plan for Ottawa betterment to himself with the certain anticipation of being completely vindicated of all charges in the end. When Washington officials complained about his extended trips to Illinois and elsewhere while on the government payroll, the former Sac and Fox agent reminded them of his prominent role in the recent Ottawa negotiations, of his wife being chronically ill from a case of "sinking chills," and when all else failed, of how niggardly he was compensated for his hard work in general. "Yes, I did leave [the agency]," he admitted in 1863, "but because of sickness and death in my family I would not take them there [to Kansas] for double the salary of an agent."[10]

The planning of a large, ornate school building, the platting of the all-important townsite, and the sale of land were proceeding at a brisk pace. Meanwhile, the rank-and-file Ottawas began to have second thoughts about their recent treaty. Impatience gave way to such open factionalism that even Jones himself began to falter. Probably because the all-important annuities were not immediately forthcoming as Hutchinson had clearly promised, the frustrated mixed-blood temporarily joined forces with a score of his recently adopted Ottawa brethren and demanded of Commissioner Dole, "What has the treaty really done for us?" Several months later, again to Dole, Jones inquired: "I am authorized by the Ottawa chief and council to ask whether Hutchinson is really our agent or not. If he is, what is he ordered to do for us?"

Conditions for the promoters deteriorated generally in 1863. Scores of starving Indians from the south invaded the Ottawa reservation, destroying crops and timber and begging for subsistence. Soldiers from nearby Civil War military installations further demoralized the Ottawas, who by now were increasingly engaged in disputes over the most valuable land and timber claims. Some even took the position that all the timber should be sold to the whites, although in retrospect this doubtlessly was a ruse to make certain claims more attractive to speculators. Even Hutchinson was beginning to have problems and was behaving erratically. Among other things, he was absent from his agency headquarters for extended periods of time, and he gave the Ottawa interpreter, Antoine Gorky, the unverified excuse for being unable to pay him that his official agency funds on deposit in a Lawrence bank had been seized by William Quantrill and his Missouri raiders.[11]

As expected, Kalloch was appointed as president of the yet-to-be-completed Indian university. The Ottawa Town Company was formally organized with Kalloch as president, Hutchinson as vice-president, and Asa Lathrop as secretary. The board membership, of course, included Ottawa Jones. To shore up the public's faltering confidence, the university board kept busy. A "timber committee" composed of Jones, Wind, Hurr, and Hutchinson was organized. The "cowardly work" of designing white men who opposed bringing the nearby Miamis under their influence was also discussed. An architect was employed, and the trinity of Jones, Kalloch, and Hutchinson applauded themselves on the encouraging letters that they were receiving from so-called Baptist benefactors in the East.

At the same time, however, the Civil War was clearly retarding the flow of settlers to the Ottawa school lands, and factionalism was giving way to open conflict among the Ottawa leadership, largely over the selection of a desirable townsite. Apparently responding to Hutchinson's arbitrary tactics with John Wilson (Partee) and several other less influential Ottawa leaders, Wilson and his supporters secured the services of Antoine Gorkey, the unpaid Ottawa interpreter, and J. F. Goodin, an attorney from nearby Minneola. In a lengthy letter to the secretary of the interior, Wilson explained that he had been an Ottawa chief and councilman for several years and that the majority of the tribe followed him. Because certain well-timbered tracts he had selected under the 1862 treaty were coveted by the town promoters, Hutchinson had refused to certify what Wilson considered his lawful claim. Instead Hutchinson had insisted that he take less-timbered lands on the north that were "wet, low and spongy." "Hutchinson said it would do no good whatsoever to oppose him," continued Wilson:

> The Secretary [of the Interior] and [Indian] Commissioner at Washington were his partners and they were going to lay out a town, and he said it would do us no good to look for a lawyer as the best lawyers on the river at Leavenworth and Lawrence were his partners in this town too, that he had been trying to bring about the [1862] treaty for two years and he had so many [Baptist] friends and the matter was tied in such a big hard knot, and so complicated, that no lawyer with *all* the Indians together could untie the knot.[12]

Informed of this, Hutchinson fought back swiftly. Describing Wilson as the only Ottawa Indian dissatisfied with his claim, the angry agent informed Commissioner Dole "that we did what we did for the best interests of the tribe." Quoting Jones, whom he lauded as the one most respected Ottawa leader, Hutchinson characterized the traditionalist Wilson as "the enemy to everything in the shape of morality, religion, or intelligence." Gorkey was depicted as "wholly treacherous and unreliable," while the attorney, Goodin, was dismissed as "a notorious drunkard" only interested in Ottawa land in general and Wilson's claim in particular. And to corroborate Hutchinson's account of what was going on among the Ottawas, Tauy Jones wrote Secretary Usher: "Wilson and his Indians are distracting us all. Bad white men are interfering with our town affairs but our agent knows what we want and no outsiders are needed. Wilson is about the laziest man in the tribe and we should not let his notions ruin us all—he is duped by wicked white men."[13]

Obviously convinced that they were being duped in a manner that threatened the best interests of the tribe as a whole, Wilson, David Barnett, and their legal advisors journeyed to Washington to press for a full-scale investigation. After their return they realized that the school lands previously purchased by Young and Kalloch at the minimum price were selling to eastern speculators at up to $3.00 per acre. They then advised Usher that such profits would allow for the construction of a $12,000 to $15,000 school. "We need no such school house," they said. "A $1,000 to $2,000 school would be ample." Of the fifty-eight Ottawa children who were to be educated and presumably sent on to the university level at some future date, twenty-four were under the influence of the town promoters, while the remaining thirty-four and their parents objected strongly to "this forced school fund which our agent is laying on us." They asked: "Are we to be kept wholly ignorant of the acts, whereabouts, and workings of our Agent? Much, most of the wrongs from which we have and are suffering have been under the cloak of religion and the feigned idea of promoting the spiritual interest of our Church." They observed that before the 1862 treaty the Ottawas had been a peaceful and united people, but now their traditional social and religious relations were "almost wholly destroyed."[14]

Under the circumstances, and in line with long-standing Indian Office tradition, Usher saw no alternative but to

send a special commissioner to the Ottawas, to determine
if fences could be mended and factional differences resolved. Selected for the task was former Central Indian
Superintendent William Albin, who arrived in Franklin
County in mid-August, 1864. He reported in January, 1865,
that there were profound differences among the Ottawa
leaders, as well as among the rank and file. Many complained of difficulty securing title to the lands that they
claimed, and confusion and concern was expressed over the
income from land sales to white settlers. In the final analysis, however, the real problem appeared to be John Wilson. "Many follow him as chief," reported Albin, "though
he holds no [official] office, yet he is unpopular with the
main body of the tribe." On the other hand, Albin was
greatly impressed with the activities of Jones, Kalloch, and
Hutchinson. To him the "main body" of the tribe was the
tribal council, and the situation in general was progressing
favorably. Albin believed that Wilson was guilty of mis-
guided obstructionism and needed to understand where
the real power in Franklin County was. Town lots had
been laid out, nearly fifty houses had been built, and more
were planned. Stores were doing a brisk business, saw-
mills were humming, and most important of all, "a 40 × 60
ft. basement had been completed at a cost of $2,000"
for the university. Evidence that Albin's basic strategy was
to pressure Wilson into accepting the new dispensation was
a letter Hutchinson wrote to Commissioner Dole following
Albin's departure from Kansas, indicating that Wilson had
expressed "regret" for his uncooperative spirit. "I welcomed
him back into the majority of the tribe," explained Hutchinson, "and have always treated him with kindness." On a
different, but no less important, area of concern, Hutchinson reported that Kalloch had talked with the Miamis, who
were indicating a serious interest in "mingling" their school
funds with the Ottawas. This was good, emphasized Hutchinson, for it would keep the Miami children "away from
the unwholesome effects of their parents, etc."[15]

By the summer of 1865 some stability appeared to have

been established in tribal affairs. Continued rumblings could be heard from the Wilson traditionalist faction, but compared to the administrative problems Agent Hutchinson was then encountering, they seemed insignificant. A warning of crisis came in August, when Hutchinson advised the newly installed Interior Secretary, Dennis N. Cooley, that he had no receipts for land sales on the Ottawa reserve because no forms for that purpose had been issued by the Indian Office. Several days later he went further by admitting that he had in his possession "only incidental or general information" regarding land transactions, again because of no forms. Responding to more certain inquiries from the Interior Department in September, Hutchinson explained that the enormous pressure of his agency responsibilities forced him to prepare his land ledgers "at odd moments of leisure." Then why, the Interior Department asked, was his agency account in a Lawrence bank running short? Because Kalloch, in his haste to catch a boat for Boston, had simply forgotten to transfer certain accounts from the ledgers of E. H. Gruber and Co., a firm in nearby Leavenworth. And why had Agent Hutchinson failed to file his annual report with Central Superintendent Thomas Murphy? The answer again was simple: Hutchinson had sent it from Vermont to his Kansas office in Ottawa, so that certain information relating to agricultural production could be included, and the report possibly was delayed or lost between New England and Kansas. Precisely what he was doing in Vermont the beleaguered Ottawa agent did not explain.[16]

It was a situation that demanded firm commitment to the grand design. Knowing full well the importance of maintaining Hutchinson's faltering credibility with the Indian Office, Reverend Kalloch worked hard to shore up his partner's poor performance. In his personally owned *Western Home Journal,* published from the frontier village of Ottawa, the Baptist promoter insisted: "It is . . . but simple justice to say that this community could not have been what it is without the efficient services which Mr. Hutch-

inson had rendered. We commend him to good men every-
where as a man to be trusted." And to reinforce his own
confidence, Kalloch resorted to the kind of pulpit persua-
sion and entrepreneural jargon that had served him so
well in the past:

> Step by step we are climbing up the steep and starry road.
> Day by day we see our cherished hopes nearing fulfillment.
> The trials of our enterprise are neither few nor small, but
> they are lost in the far more exceeding reward of laboring in
> so grand a work. When we see what has been wrought in
> the last two years we are filled with amazement and grati-
> tude. Two years hence, we confidently predict, will witness
> still greater changes and more rapid progress.[17]

Reverend Isaac McCoy. (Except where indicated, the illustrations on these pages are reproduced courtesy of the Kansas State Historical Society, Topeka.)

Reverend Jotham Meeker

John Tecumseh (Tauy) Jones, sometimes also known as
Ottawa Jones.

Clinton C. Hutchinson

Reverend Isaac Kalloch

OTAWA

MUSENAIKUN.

EUE KO

WLKI UKENOUMATEWIN;

KUER ANINT

OMIN'WAHIMOWIN NOK,

KAPWA OLEPEUMOWAT

MRTO KUER HAN;

KUER OTAWAK

OTEPAKONIKRWINIWAN.

UWI TUL

WRLTOT UHIHAK,

RNONIKOHIN

KEHIMOKOMANEWE PRPTISUN.

Nalif Wrlhikatrk.

Otawa Prptise Kukekwrwikumikof.

UHIHAK, MRSENAIKUNIKRT,

1850.

The text on the book cover shown here reads, "Ottawa First Book, Containing Lessons for the reader, Portions of the Gospel Omitted by Matthew and John, and the Ottawa Laws, by Joth Meeker, Missionary of the American Baptist Mission Union; Second Edition, Ottawa Baptist Mission Station, J. Meeker, Printer, 1850."

Main Street, Ottawa, Kansas, 1866.

An early twentieth-century photograph of Tauy Jones Hall, the original Ottawa Indian University building constructed in the late 1860s.

Home of Tauy Jones, constructed in the 1860s about 3¼ miles northeast of Ottawa, Kansas.

Grave of Compchau (Kom-Chaw), just northeast of Ottawa. Kom-Chaw was one of the Ottawa chiefs who came under the influence of the non-Indian promoters of the Ottawa Indian University.

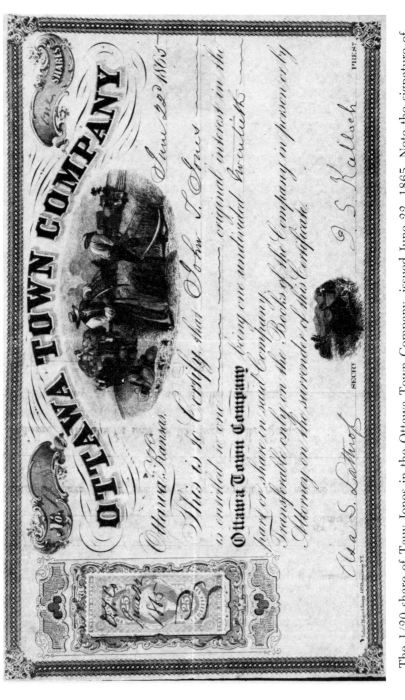

The 1/20 share of Tauy Jones in the Ottawa Town Company, issued June 22, 1865. Note the signature of "I. S. Kalloch, Pres." *(Courtesy Archives and Special Collections, Ottawa University Library)*

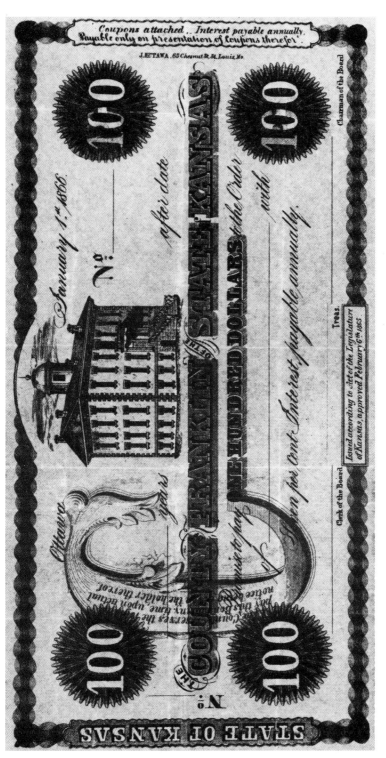

Franklin County bond, issued January 1, 1866, showing the original university building before it was gutted by fire. (*Courtesy Archives and Special Collections, Ottawa University Library*)

6

The Perils of Providence

THE SERIOUS investigation by the Interior Department of the complex university land scheme began while the plan was still in the process of fruition, thus creating the necessity for a defense amid the offense. W. R. Irwin, dispatched by the Interior Department in March, 1867, to have another look at the university construction, the townsite, and the land allotments, reported to Secretary Orville Browning that there might be good reasons why the furor among the Ottawas had not died down.

Irwin examined Hutchinson with a thoroughness that revealed weaknesses that apparently had not been evident to Albin earlier. For one thing, it was confirmed that Hutchinson was indeed a very poor keeper of records. No regular books had been kept, and the evidence of land sales made by the agent consisted of entries in memorandum books, rough copies of reports to the Interior Department, and duplicates of receipts, all of which were "in a state of confusion and full of mistakes and discrepencies." Part of the work had been done by Hutchinson and part by clerks during the long periods when he had been absent, but it was clear to Irwin that it would be "a long and complicated piece of work, requiring care and patience, to unravel the whole matter and arrive at the facts." It appears that at this juncture Washington officials had made a determination that they would, whatever the effort, sort out the facts about the Ottawa reserve.

Irwin talked seriously with Hutchinson about the latter's responsibility to the government and to the Indians for any money that might remain in his possession. The agent said he would be unable to pay any shortage at present, but would turn over the papers and pay the balance eventually. He did not, however, say what disposition had been made of the money or when he would pay. He only hinted that he would have an explanation to make when his accounts were adjusted and the balance due from him was ascertained. Those explanations were unacceptable to Irwin, and in April, 1867, Hutchinson was suspended as Ottawa agent, though he was not allowed to resign formally for fear that he might ultimately escape accountability. It was planned that the separate Ottawa Agency would be allowed to pass out of existence, making the Sac and Fox agent responsible for final collections on the lands that Hutchinson had sold. That was done, but not before Isaac Kalloch applied, in February, 1867, for appointment as Hutchinson's successor at the Ottawa Agency. His application was quickly denied.[1]

The Irwin report of March 6 and the investigator's continual prying into the records of area banks through April and May in search of Hutchinson's lost funds occasioned considerable activity on the part of the university trustees. Kalloch wrote to the Office of Indian Affairs late in March that he was an honest man who had acted "with an eye single to the reimbursement of the Government and the protection of the school," yet he was being treated as though he were a criminal in league with Hutchinson. His complete innocence of any scheme perpetuated by Hutchinson was, according to Kalloch, demonstrated by his pledge to Indian Commissioner Lewis Bogy and Senator Samuel Pomeroy that, were he allowed to manage the matter until the following July, he would pay the former agent's debt. An investigation would publicize irregularities in the university's administration and make it impossible to collect funds from the school's friends in the East. It would also make it difficult to pay Hutchinson's debt, since the agent had no other source of funds. On May 7, Irwin reported to Browning that of the $45,000 that Hutchinson admitted receiving from land sales, $31,103.94 was unaccounted for, and that after learning of Irwin's visits to banks in Lawrence and Leavenworth, Hutchinson and his wife had conveyed to the Interior Department as security for this debt all of their real estate except their house. This real estate consisted of town lots and farms worth about $15,000. On that same May 7 the University Board of Trustees heard a statement concerning Hutchinson's debts, and it voted to write the Interior Department requesting it to grant the board a reasonable time to aid in their payment and therefore avoid damage to the university's reputation. The letter was sent immediately.[2]

The principals under investigation did not, however, conduct themselves in a manner that was calculated to reduce the governmental pressure. That is, they did not refrain from their possibly fraudulent activities. Kalloch admitted that the University Board was continuing to sell school and trust lands beyond those that had been authorized in the 1862 treaty, in anticipation of a clause authorizing some selling that was to be included in a new treaty, then under consideration. He also insisted that the board had been unable to find the proper agent at the time when it was selling and, since his map had many faded colors, he had been unable to get accurate descriptions; but with opportunity knocking and the university in financial distress, the lands had been sold for $1.50, a little above their appraised value. These were, in Kalloch's evaluation, marginal lands that could be sold only to friends of the university interested in a philanthropy. Therefore he trusted that the Indian Office would regard this technically illegal device of unauthorized sales as a legitimate method of aiding an institution that needed all the help it could get. Although Hutchinson and Kalloch both resigned from the Board of Trustees during the period of the Irwin revelations, apparently it was not from their own sense of misconduct. Kalloch left first, late in April, 1867, and his position was filled by the Reverend R. Jeffrey of Philadelphia, who was guaranteed the chance to buy 320 acres of land at $2.50. Then on May 7, Hutchinson resigned, the election of Jeffrey was rescinded, and Kalloch was reinstated (although he would again resign in the near future).

To understand the reasons for these maneuvers is at best difficult. When Hutchinson's town property was transferred, complaints were filed by city residents that the agent had sold lots after he had agreed to turn them over to the Interior Department, and that, in the process, businessmen already located upon these lots were denied a chance to buy from the government. Meanwhile, Hutchinson removed to a farm, which he bought through the kindness of a friend who advanced $500, and proceeded to try to satisfy the obligations against him. He complained that he was virtually excluded from all business except manual labor and that he was hard pressed to support his family. He said he hoped his attempt to pay his accounts in full by the sale of his property would dispel the "undesirable disgrace" from his name. Certainly he did not at this time deny that he owed a large sum of money to the government.[3]

The uncertain relationship of the Board of Trustees to its own members and the failure to acknowledge any fraud in the land speculation, together with accompanying suspicion of possible undue influence upon the treaty process, were possibly the reasons why the treaty with the Ottawas and other tribes signed February 23, 1867, was not ratified until more than a year later. By the 1862 treaty the original 74,000 acres of Ottawa lands had been divided into three categories: 20,000 acres of "school lands"; 30,000 acres of trust lands that the Ottawas ceded for sale to settlers through their agent, Hutchinson; and approximately 24,000 acres of allotments to individual Ottawas. In the 1867 treaty the tribe agreed to remove south to the Indian Territory (the future state of Oklahoma). It authorized the use of part of the money that had been held by the United States from sale of the Ottawas' trust lands since 1862 to buy for their occupation the west part of the Shawnee Reservation in Indian Territory at $1.00 an acre. The rest of those funds were to be held for their benefit. The allotments were individually titled to tribal members, who could do with them what they would. Most were sold when the tribe removed, thus providing, together with the 7,000 acres of trust lands remaining unsold in 1867, a 31,000-acre base for the long-expected second phase of the grand scheme—which was the formation of a land speculation company upon the nonschool portion of the Ottawa lands, whose principal officers would hold interlocking positions in the university and townsite speculations.

What had been pressed informally to the limits of plausibility and far beyond legality now became possible on a legitimate basis, but at a time when the promoters, hampered by investigations of their past activities, were burdened with more constraints in future planning than they had anticipated. There was still hope, however. The time period during which individual Ottawas were allowed to declare themselves citizens of the United States and sever their tribal relation was extended by the new treaty from July 16, 1867, to July 16, 1869. This provision could be interpreted as working to the advantage of those trying to operate a speculation based upon tribal authority and the manipulation of factions. Meanwhile, the claim of Jones for the destruction of his propery in 1856 was allowed in the amount of $6,700, to the evident joy of his many creditors.[4]

Regarding the university, there were three important changes in the 1867 treaty. First, all children of the Ottawa tribe between the ages of six and eighteen were to receive free schooling and were to be subsisted, clothed, and provided with medical care at the institution's expense. This provision was to ensure that the movement of the tribe did not deny its children the education for which they had paid. Second, the secretary of the interior and the senior corresponding secretary of the American Baptist Home Mission were made ex officio members of the University Board of Trustees in order to "furnish additional supervision of the institution, so that the provisions of this article may be carried into effect in their full spirit and intent." There was reason to doubt that this had been the case in the past. Last, and more acceptable to the schemers, it was agreed that the unsold portion of the trust lands should be sold to the trustees of Ottawa University. They were to be purchased by the board at their appraised value and used for the benefit of the institution.[5] Thanks to the untiring activities of Hutchinson these lands amounted to only 7,221 acres in 1867.

The university experienced little difficulty adjusting to those conditions, since its own interest had always been carefully examined in regard to trust land sales even before the treaty provision was inserted. Indeed, its board could hardly wait for its actions to be fully legalized by the ratification of the treaty before beginning the sale of the final 7,000 acres. Kalloch, in November, 1867, asked Commissioner of Indian Affairs Charles Mix to rule that, in order to complete the elaborate university building that fall, it would be necessary to sell these lands before treaty ratification. Again, he resorted to the "cloak of religion." It was "not for speculation but benevolence" that the board again requested permission to violate the letter of the law, because the 7,000 acres comprised the worst land of the trust lands, and these lands might not sell at all if the board were not given a free hand to populate the area with whites.

With an expensive building going up, a fine orchard in the making, and substantial obligations to eastern investors, the university was beginning to take on the image of an established community fixture. It had erected temporary buildings in town at a cost of $5,000 and claimed to be feeding and clothing fifty Ottawa children at an annual expense of $3,000. In fact, it may have been doing just about what the treaties authorized it to do, except that the

loan fund for agricultural improvement had not been established. According to the 1862 treaty, this fund was to
have been established from the proceeds of the 15,000
acres of school lands remaining after the university took
its previously determined 5,000-acre share. The money
that the loan fund was to have provided for Ottawa farmers
had been expended on a new building, appointments, cur-
riculum development, and perhaps a portion of the townsite. This was in direct violation of the 1862 treaty.[6]

As the federal government moved to institute a suit
against Hutchinson's property, the residents of Ottawa defended the university, but later reneged when their support
was demanded in the form of hard cash rather than negotiations with competing Indian factions. In the summer of
1867, Kalloch's *Western Home Journal* complained about
"lewd fellows of the baser sort" who were trying to cripple
the progress of the university, and compared such to swine
whose "home is in the gutter and their food is dirt." Yet
a year later, when the college asked the town to issue
$6,000 worth of bonds to support the college, previous
articles about the institution providing jobs and promoting
growth were notably absent. The editorials in June, 1868,
took the theme that colleges did little toward building up
towns, and that with an endowment such as the university
had from the Indians, it should not have to come begging
to anyone. This change in the relationship of the townsite
and the school may have occurred because in February,
1868, Kalloch was permanently removed from the University Board of Trustees. Thus both Hutchinson and Kalloch,
the founders of the townsite, had involuntarily severed
their formal connection with the university.[7]

Kalloch's demise as board member was a consequence
of the arrival in Ottawa in January, 1868, of the Reverend
Robert Atkinson, who had been newly appointed by the
Baptist Home Mission Society as its district secretary for
Kansas and adjoining regions. In late January, Atkinson
addressed the board, which was then composed of Pratt,
Kalloch, Jones, King, Wind, and Hurr, and explained the

resolve of the Home Mission Society to aid Ottawa University and make it into a Baptist institution. Pratt then made a motion, which Jones seconded, that Atkinson be made a member of the board to replace Hutchinson. The motion carried unanimously. Atkinson was also appointed treasurer and secretary of the board and given authority to consult immediately with the Kansas State Baptist Convention.[8]

Atkinson was a man of importance who combined a reputation for "spotless integrity" with a background which made it evident that he was not immune to the appeal of the dollar—a combination well suited for the Ottawa speculation at this critical point in its development. Born in 1824, he had attended Madison (now Coalgate) University, where he probably had come to know Ottawa Jones. Subsequently, he had spent eleven years as pastor of the North Church of Newark, New Jersey, where he had demonstrated his financial prowess by raising $65,000 within the congregation's ranks for the erection of a large church building. This activity, combined with his temperance and mission work, had led to his appointment to the board of the Baptist Home Mission Society and eventually to his great challenge at Ottawa. The society, it was later said, realized in 1868 that the affairs of the university in the West "were daily growing more complicated" and required that "a master mind must take affairs in hand." Atkinson seemed just the man. He was a businessman, holding stock in a braid-manufacturing establishment in Passaic, New Jersey; a religious leader, who continued to teach Bible classes; and an astute evaluator of political trends, who was to be elected three times to the Ottawa City Council and who met personally with President Ulysses S. Grant during the Ottawa crisis, all the while claiming that he had no desire to identify himself with politics. He was, as one writer has suggested, the Baptist "Man of the Hour."[9]

On February 17 the Kansas State Baptist Convention held a joint meeting with the University Board in Lawrence to confirm the new relationship. There it was determined that Hutchinson had sold 3,000 acres of school land without the authority of the trustees and at prices far below the real value, while Kalloch had done the same with 2,872 acres. In effect admitting to this, Kalloch proposed to the convention that, if it would now ratify all the sales he had made, he would drop his various claims against the trustees for expenses. The Baptist Convention recommended that this be done, while it advised that Hutchinson's actions remain a charge against him. At a board meeting in Lawrence immediately after the joint meeting, Treasurer Atkinson was authorized not only to ratify the sales of land made by Kalloch (and not those made by Hutchinson) but also to give Kalloch a deed to lands that Kalloch claimed to have purchased from Hutchinson. When this was done, Kalloch tendered his resignation for the second time.[10]

A more direct role of the Baptists in the support and administration of the University had been established by the clause in the 1867 treaty giving them ex officio representation on the board, but the arrival of Atkinson and the subsequent reorientation of the board after his investigation of the affairs of Hutchinson and Kalloch represented a watershed in the history of the Ottawa fraud. Certain obvious questions arise regarding the situation as it stood early in 1868. Did it represent an attempt at reform? A new speculation scheme? A modified version of the old plan with new beneficiaries? Merely an attempt by the Baptists to protect an enterprise with which they had been involved from the beginning? Was Hutchinson being used as a scapegoat by the new board to divert the federal investigators? What leverage did Kalloch enjoy that he was not similarly treated?

Certainly there were marked changes. Most striking, the University Board of Trustees did not meet at all from the time of the joint convention until it met in the Baptist church at Lawrence in mid-January, 1869, almost a year later. In the interim Atkinson went east to try to raise money, and an Ottawa delegation followed him in an attempt to negotiate a new treaty. No new board member was elected to fill Kalloch's place during this period, as it was uncertain whether trustee Pratt would move to Ottawa, and Atkinson wanted at least one member living outside the area. Also, Pratt was busy moving the Delawares south to the Indian Territory and so could not attend any meetings to provide the legal quorum of the two white members. On the other hand, Atkinson did admit that due to his fund-raising travels he was seldom in Ottawa. He wrote to Indian Commissioner N. G. Taylor in February, 1869, that during this time he had communicated often with the Indian trustees and that they were satisfied, both by his action against Hutchinson and Kalloch and by the action that the board took when it finally did meet to provide $3,000 a year for the education of Ottawa children. Atkinson suggested that this last policy was an especially generous action, clearly beyond the minimum support that the board was obliged by treaty to provide. In response, Chief Wilson expressed grave concern whether the Ottawas would enjoy the educational benefits that they had bargained for, once they had moved south. The board therefore agreed to the $3,000 fund "to be given when it [could] be realized as interest on moneys received from the sail [sic] of college lands." In the meantime the board had decided to ask the Baptists for help with their educational enterprise. Atkinson felt that additional concern about the Indians was unneccessary because the elegant school building (in the future known as Tauy Jones hall) had more than compensated the tribe for its original gift of lands, by increasing the value of those lands remaining to them and by bringing them "civilization."[11]

The long-delayed 1869 meeting was made more stormy because Hutchinson made a serious attempt to be reinstated on the University Board. Hutchinson worked among the Indians to obtain their support for putting him in Kalloch's vacant place among the trustees, thus pursuing vengeance for the ill will that he felt when the board had dismissed him without a word of concern a year earlier.

Atkinson learned just in time of a plan to hold a board meeting in his absence that might elect Hutchinson. From Tauy Jones Hall he wrote Secretary of the Interior Browning that, if Hutchinson succeeded and a "true man" was thus denied the place, the affairs of the university would be so deeply jeopardized as to be inextricable. Atkinson succeeded in setting the meeting at a time convenient to himself and to his plan to control the ex officio proxies.[12]

Many members of the Ottawa tribe interpreted the events of 1868 and early 1869 in a less favorable light than Atkinson did. Their representatives went to Washington to seek a new treaty and a fresh start. In the first place, they were frightened that their removal from Kansas would mean the end of their educational privileges at Ottawa University. John Wilson, who along with Wind, Hurr, and King formed the delegation to Washington, had to plead with the board and finally threaten it with a new treaty, to achieve even a modest agreement to provide support for Indian students at the university. Even then the board would only guarantee that support if the sales of former Indian lands warranted it. Yet the 1867 treaty had stated that all expenses for all Ottawa children presenting themselves for education should be paid by the university as long as any should appear there, and it was upon that condition that the Ottawas had agreed to remove at all.

In addition to the board's reluctance to honor those obligations, the Ottawas complained that the new $50,000 building had in fact been designed as a school for whites, and that neither the expense of it nor the use of it for anything other than an Indian school were ever permitted by treaty agreements with them. As a consequence, some members of the tribe in 1867 refused to send their children to school, and at the board meeting of February 11, 1868, school activities were suspended altogether. According to the board, there was a mutual agreement to suspend classes until the new building could be completed. The board insisted that, when the building was finished on March 11, 1869, an invitation was issued to the Ottawas to attend, but that they were then influenced by "designing white men" and refused.

Meanwhile, the Ottawa delegation pressed for a provision in any new treaty that would direct the sale of the university and its lands and the distribution of the proceeds directly to the Ottawa tribe. In their view, the school was doing nothing for the tribe. The delegation thought that the land adjoining the college might sell for as much as $150 an acre and that the building itself would go for $35,000, making a possible total payment to the tribe of over $200,000, even after deducting the $7,000 owed to the Baptists. The tribe said it would sell to the Baptists or to anyone else. It questioned Atkinson's estimate that the land was worth no more than $25,000 and that the Baptists had contributed over $30,000 to its development. Of course, the university had done much for the town, the Ottawas admitted, and of course, it had increased the value of their remaining lands—this they had expected when they had set aside the original 20,000 acres. But why did Atkinson speak of the land as a "gift" when that word did not appear in any of the treaties? And why should the Ottawas be required to subsidize white education and townsite speculation when the goal of the land division had been the education of their children "not to be thereafter taken away from us by any company, corporation, church or association"?

> Mr. Atkinson in his last appeal says Justice to the people of Ottawa. Justice to the people of the surrounding country. Justice to the denomination that have made so large donations but no prayer for Justice to the poor Indian. This seems to be a one side affair. Now cannot these true Philanthropists who have satisfied much of the comforts of civilization and refinement and gave forth as missionaries to civilize, educate, enlighten and christianize the poor Indian see no justice for him? [13]

The defense of the board was that, whatever its indiscretions in the past, it had purged itself of those evil men and that that degraded, speculating clique, full of sour grapes, was now working on the other side of the issue by attempting to influence the Ottawas to press for university confiscation. It denied the Indians' argument that, because the original white trustees were elected by the Indian trustees and not by the tribe as a whole, the board was never legally constituted according to treaty and that all its actions were void. That argument turned upon the meaning of the term "said Ottawas" in the 1862 treaty, which was a phrase subject to varying interpretations. The board also denied the contention that it had delayed a year in replacing Kalloch because there were no good men left in Ottawa. Certainly Kalloch's replacement, J. S. Emory, was a good man.[14]

Still there were bad men about. In March, 1869, C. N. Blacklidge, an attorney for the tribe, came forth with the argument that in the spring of 1866, when there had been promises of immediate aid from wealthy people in the East, Hutchinson had used about $30,000 or more of the Indian funds that were entrusted to him as their agent, and perhaps some proceeds from land sales that were not authorized officially by the board, to pay the bills due to contractors for building, labor, and materials. This argument was the origin of Hutchinson's subsequent contention that he had used this money "for the benefit of the Ottawas" and not his own and therefore had no obligation to repay the government. It was also the beginning of the rapprochement of the antiboard faction of the tribe with Hutchinson, whose interest now was to destroy the new board, especially if in doing so he could cash in his attorney's fees and could, in exchange for his aid, elicit from the Ottawas a favorable confirmation of his past actions.

Atkinson characterized Hutchinson's double dealings as "sophistry and fraud" and asserted that this "malicious spirit" had hoodwinked everyone in the past and was attempting to do it again in his new guise as a friend to the poor Indian. "His whole past history shows him to be an unjust man." S. S. Beroker, writing in March, 1869, on behalf of the Baptists, likewise argued that all the problems in Ottawa could be traced to Hutchinson's using his position and patronage to speculate in Indian lands, and that it was Hutchinson's bitterness at being caught with his hand in the till, as well as his unwillingness to pay the wages of sin, that were responsible for the sudden discovery by the Ottawas that they were unjustly served by the Baptists and the University Board. The board was shocked and amazed that a new treaty was even being considered, and it was pleased when both Interior Secretary Orville Browning and his successor, J. D. Cox, were cool to the idea. "Shall a new treaty be made to gratify these unreasonable men, which shall break up the present board? . . . We claim we have vested rights."[15]

What was meant by "vested rights" quickly became obvious. Atkinson moved his family into the university building, which boasted such refinements as mahogany woodwork and a rosewood piano. Even in 1984, though several fires had gutted the interior, the craftsmanship and expense of the exterior stonework of three-story Tauy Jones Hall were still evident to the visitor. Under Atkinson's direction a room was set aside in which the female teachers could live protected from any unfriendly Indians or trustees who might be lurking about, an official seal was adopted, and a college farm and nursery were established on a fenced tract one mile square surrounding the building. The citizens of the town had in a public meeting expressed surprise and concern that the school was not really in control of the Baptists at all, but a "close corporation" run by a few individuals. Atkinson addressed the board on several occasions to counter that view by outlining the "true history" of Ottawa University and by noting that the new Leavenworth, Lawrence, and Galveston railroad would soon bring substantial dividends and growth to Franklin County. The "Euphemian" undergraduate debating society at the school meanwhile addressed such timely questions as "Is a lawyer justified in defending a person whom he knows to be guilty?" or "Resolved: There is more pleasure in pursuit than possession."[16]

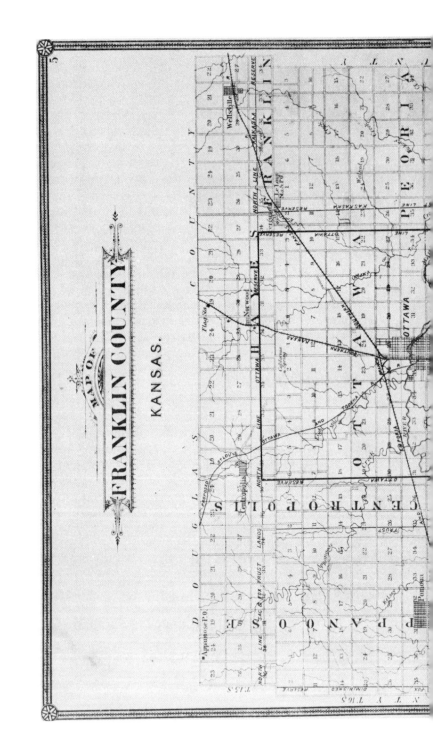

MAP OF
FRANKLIN COUNTY.
KANSAS.

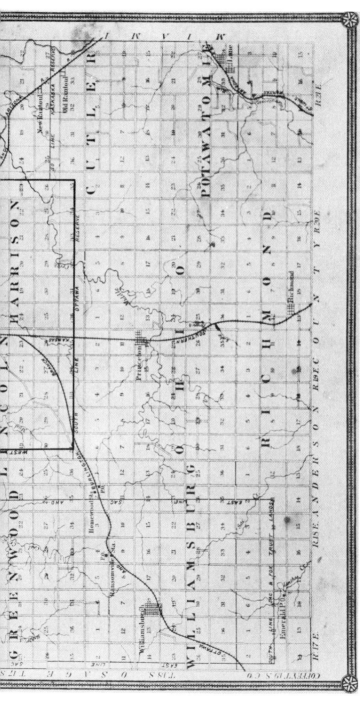

Franklin County, Kansas. Reproduced from *Historical Atlas of Franklin County, Kansas* (Chicago: Davy Map and Atlas Co., 1885), courtesy of Department of Special Collections, Wichita State University Library. The precise location of Ottawa Indian University is in Section 36, T 16 S, R 19 E.

Late in the spring of 1869 complications developed outside the board to counterbalance the complications within. Certain Ottawas belonging to the long-dissident Wilson faction, believing that the Board of Trustees had never been legally constituted, elected a separate and competing board, whose white members were the attorney Blacklidge and former Kansas Governor Wilson Shannon. Also backing this maverick board were C. C. Hutchinson and S. A. Riggs, a former U.S. district attorney for Kansas. At the same time the Ottawa tribe (or at least the Wilson faction, which claimed to be the majority) issued a receipt to the former agent relieving him in full from the $41,993 obligation the Indian Office had determined Hutchinson owed them as a result of fraud. The Indian Office did not recognize this receipt, and much information was yet to come regarding the methods Hutchinson and his friends had used in acquiring it. Nevertheless, suddenly there it was, signed April 15 and delivered to Washington soon after. The final blow in this episode was a meeting of the Ottawa general council on April 24, 1869, which excluded university promoter Tauy Jones from membership in the tribe. The resolution stated that, though Jones had been with them for twenty years, he "has by his conduct during the last few months shown himself to be no longer identified with us and our interests." Jones and his wife were denied the right to receive any money paid to the tribe, and he was refused the privilege of speaking for the tribe either in Washington or at meetings of the University Board of Trustees, of which he remained a member until his death in 1872.[17]

Jones and Atkinson, the most articulate of those who were outraged by this remarkable series of occurrences, bombarded Washington with letters of protest. Jones wrote that Hutchinson had "duped and persuaded our people that he put that amount [the $41,993] in the school house." This Hutchinson categorically denied. According to Jones, Hutchinson had become active in 1868, holding secret meetings with a number of influential people both in Ot-

tawa and Washington. The Indians apparently were persuaded that, if Hutchinson were freed of his debt, he could
lead them to greater riches by destroying the board and
forcing the sale of the value-inflated buildings and lands.
Jones went on to say that Hutchinson was privately talking
about a new treaty which would establish a new board,
make him president with full power to choose the other
board members, and accept as a buyer for the property the
Episcopal Church, which had an under-the-table agreement with Jay Cooke and Company to create a speculation
more lucrative than the one underway.

Atkinson was just as agitated. While he was confident
that such developments could not damage the board, he
was equally sure they would embarrass it in trying to sell
their lands. Hutchinson had made threats. He claimed that,
since he had written most of the treaty in 1862, he knew
of some wording, notably that referring to "said Ottawa
Indians," which could "upset the school" if interpreted in
a certain way. Hutchinson said that he had promised not to
bring up the question of the legal constitution of the board
as long as the board would refuse to assist the government
investigation of him by providing damaging records and
information. When the board did provide some vouchers
and accounts, Hutchinson had developed a counterstrategy
to destroy it. Riggs, said Atkinson, had joined the maverick
board because he felt "sore" toward the government for
dismissing him from his district attorney post and toward
the board for giving information to aid in that dismissal
(in fact, he had conspired with Hutchinson in a court case
against the board). The young men in the tribe told the
board that the Ottawas had agreed to pay "Blacklige &
Co." $10,000 if they could turn the old board out and sell
the property.

On July 15, 1869, Jones wrote to Indian Commissioner
E. S. Parker, himself a Seneca Indian, that he hoped the
present attorney general of Kansas was, unlike Riggs, an
honest man and would investigate the whole matter. Continued Jones,

I desire you as a friend to the Indians to look into this attempt of fraud on its naked and hard face and turn it over and over until you shall have seen the monster demon in it and cast it off as St. Paul cast off the snake or serpent into the fire. It is too bad to see men engage in such nefarious business.[18]

7

Machinations Magnified

By 1869 most investigating agencies concerned with Ottawa University, including the Board of Indian Commissioners, had concluded, as one official wrote, "A full investigation of this scheme will . . . convince you that it is designed to enable some of these men to *cover up* some of their *corrupt transactions* while they held office under the U.S. Government & at the same time to swindle the Indians and enrich themselves." The investigative proceedings in that year took on a more serious tone. There were attacks on the entrenched boards, old and new, on two fronts. First, Hutchinson was brought into court on charges of defrauding the government and the Indians. His case dragged on into 1872 through several mistrials and, thanks to the continued dexterity of Hutchinson, created in the process almost as many actions of questionable legality as the situation that had prompted legal charges in the first place. The Indian Office also held hearings in the Office of Central Superintendent Enoch Hoag in Lawrence. Neither action resulted in any significant punishment for the schemers. Incredibly, the Hutchinson case was settled out of court in exchange for a nominal sum ($1,000) paid into the U.S. Treasury by Hutchinson. The $41,993.71 voucher issue was pursued no further.[1]

In the autumn of 1869 the District Court of Kansas

declared that, since it believed Hutchinson had put the unaccounted-for money ($41,993.71) into the university building, it was spent for the benefit of the Ottawas and therefore no illegal action was involved. A new trial, however, was granted upon the technicality raised by the district attorney that the voucher given to Hutchinson by the Ottawas, affirming that the Indians approved this diversion of funds after the fact, had not been acted upon by the secretary of the interior. The commissioner of Indian affairs argued that the statement of the Indians was not evidence and that they could not execute any paper that would impair the rights of the United States to act as their guardian in collecting from Hutchinson. The commissioner noted that the proceeds from the land that Hutchinson had sold were, according to the treaties, not applicable to the erection of the university building. Only the proceeds from the 5,000 acres for which specific treaty provision had been made could legally have been used for that purpose. No loan fund had been established with the income from the remaining 15,000 acres of school lands, from which the interest might have been used; and proceeds from the sale of trust lands were to be held for the Ottawas by the United States, not Hutchinson. District Attorney Albert Horton told the court that the plaintiff had not had time to prepare a case before the first trial and that the attorney acting for the United States in that trial had acted in collusion with Hutchinson's attorneys to defraud the government. That attorney was S. A. Riggs, who subsequently had become a member of Hutchinson's new University Board. Although the court first ruled against a new trial, the evidence of collusion among the attorneys, not to mention new evidence regarding the issue at hand, was so overwhelming that a retrial was at last granted.[2]

Hutchinson inveighed against Atkinson and the old board with a vengeance, as the original alliance under heavy pressure finally crumbled. He was, he said, being used as a cat's paw by the Baptists who had loaded him like the scapegoat with their collected sins and were now driving him over the cliff. In October, 1869, Hutchinson wrote a long letter of defense to Secretary of the Interior J. D. Cox in which he gave his version of the events surrounding the founding of the university and its subsequent development. He argued that the school was never intended as a small school merely for Ottawa children but as an Indian university to which the Miamis, Potawatomis, and other tribes expected to send their children. He had deferred reporting that he had used money in his keeping to forward that goal by contributing to the building because Kalloch had convinced him to keep quiet, for fear that the Baptists in the East would be frightened off by knowledge of the university's financial troubles. Kalloch had assured the agent that money would come from the East to pay Hutchinson back for his advances and the discrepancy would never be known. "My pride, my ambition, as well as my sense of duty was in the University," wrote the former agent. "I went into the Ottawa business not to make money, but to make the best college and the best Colony in the West. Rather than injure the Institution I was willing to suffer in silence, confident that in due time justice would vindicate itself."

Hutchinson claimed that he had never taken an action injurious to the Indians and that the only Indians complaining were those influenced by Jones, who had been thrown out of the tribe. The "venom that so readily drips from the pen of the Rev. Robt. Atkinson and his friends whenever mentioning my name" was explained by their fears that he might reveal their own parts in the affair. These "gentlemen whose pious indignation overflows in such elegant terms whenever my wicked name is mentioned" had themselves wanted the university buildings for the Baptists and wanted the grounds free from Indian influence altogether. When the Roger Williams University had been organized in the early sixties, it had not an acre of land, nor a volume for the library, "nor a shingle or nail for the building." For that they now owed a profound debt to the tribe, which the former agent, from his altered perspective outside the combination of power, well recognized.[3]

The investigation conducted by Central Superintendent Enoch Hoag in Lawrence lasted from December 1, 1869, to January 11, 1870, and turned up a remarkable amount of information from all parties. Hoag came to believe that at the time John W. Young resigned from the University Board and was replaced by I. S. Kalloch, the board had begun to betray the trust conferred upon it by the treaty of 1862. The testimony made it clear that the tribe had not intended that the school use any more than the 5,000 acres for buildings, but it was also clear that the Indian members of the board, "having little confidence in their own capacity," gave authority to transact business exclusively to Hutchinson and Kalloch. On May 1, 1864, a building committee had been appointed composed of Hutchinson, Jones, and Pratt. Pratt, then with the Delawares, was a silent partner, and the character of Jones was already under suspicion. The 5,000 acres sold to Young for $6,250 had provided (at inflated Civil War prices) only enough money for the basement of the university structure. Even then the Ottawas had perceived that something was wrong, and they had complained in visits to the site that the basement (65 × 45 feet) was much too large. They had been assured that friends in the East would pay for the superstructure, but the repeated trips east had resulted only in expenses, no donations. Kalloch, however, had insisted in conversations with the board that money would be forthcoming, and contracts were let for further building.

As it happened, the whole cost of the walls ($10,770) and the carpentry ($12,554) was paid with land-sale receipts in Hutchinson's keeping. Hutchinson, it was learned, was in a three-year period following the treaty of July, 1862, selling both school lands and trust lands, giving each buyer of prairie trust land the option of a timber plot from the school reserve. Although the agent argued before Hoag at the hearing that it would have been impossible to sell trust lands without this device, the superintendent concluded this was a gross violation of the trust and that it was easy to understand why Hutchinson had been unable to keep accurate accounts. In fact, Hutchinson had signed blank deeds and left them in the charge of his clerks while he went east searching for money and emigrants. The clerks had used the funds gained to pay contractors, and Kalloch had sometimes borrowed from them, saying confidently that he would repay from moneys coming out of the East before Hutchinson returned. At one point Hutchinson became desperate and ordered the building stopped, since he was advancing part of his salary and funds raised on his personal property, as well as Indian funds, to keep it going. The board at that point brought up the question of Hutchinson's deficiencies. He was then ousted, and the Reverend Robert Atkinson arrived upon the scene. The Ottawas had opposed the treaty of 1867, according to their testimony before Hoag, and had feared that their removal south would strip them of all interest in, or control over, the university. No matter how forcefully the Reverend Atkinson might argue that he had raised the funds with which the building was completed, the fact remained that he was employed and paid by the Board of Trustees, whose duties and powers were strictly defined by the 1862 treaty. "His time was theirs," concluded Hoag, "and unless he can show, as he fails to do, that said subscriptions, or any part thereof, were given for purposes foreign to the provisions of the . . . 6th Art. of treaty of 1862, I can see no good and valid reason why they should not be applied to the purposes provided in said article." Yet, if the amounts that Atkinson claimed he had raised had in fact gone into the building, they would have very nearly covered the costs. What then had happened to the cash from the sale of the Ottawas' land?[4]

The official testimony revealed further irregularities, but Hoag was reluctant to discuss those in his report. After all, the Quaker superintendent had been representing the secretary of the interior on the University Board since 1868 and, as was later shown, had been influential in convincing the tribe to give Hutchinson a receipt for the $41,993.71. There is every evidence that Hoag was the best friend Hutchinson had in the enterprise and that he tried to minimize the agent's guilt by suggesting the complicity of Kalloch and the clerks, as well as by raising the possibility that the Baptists were not without responsibility. Even so, Hutchinson's testimony during the hearings could only be described as evasive.

Hutchinson rested his defense upon the receipt that he held from the Ottawas and refused to discuss anything else. He especially refused to answer any question put to him by John T. Jones. Others, however, revealed damaging things about him. He had been gone east promoting his townsite interests for fully ten months during the critical period of university construction, and while the school and trust lands, for which he as agent was responsible, were selling at a rapid rate. In addition to the university, two other temporary schoolhouses had been built, one costing $700 and the other $3,000. Jones claimed that these were paid for from the 5,000-acre school land sale, but Hutchinson claimed they were paid for with money advanced by him to Kalloch—from what fund he did not explain.

Hutchinson was much more talkative in responding to other witnesses than in his own testimony. He testified that at a meeting at Jones's store on January 1, 1864, the tribe had given him full power to expend money and "to travel and employ agents and clerks, to carry out the objects contemplated in our enterprise at Ottawa." He argued that he had had firm pledges of $15,000 from people in Philadelphia which were "suddenly withdrawn." No documentation of either claim was submitted, though he said that in the first case the Indians had signed a paper. When the fund-raising campaign had failed, the agent had drawn up a congressional bill giving 200,000 acres of public lands to Ottawa University for experiments in the growth of forest trees and hedges on the Kansas plains. He thought he was performing a fine service with this, but Congress had adjourned without taking action on the bill. He had sent Kalloch more than $4,000, which he claimed were proceeds from the sale of his house and lots in Ottawa; and also, admittedly, more blank deeds. Hutchinson denied that he had authorized the investment of receipts from trust-land sales in the building, but he admitted that they had in fact been spent for that purpose. Neither Hutchinson nor Atkinson were able to produce a subscription list demonstrating that a single cent had come from Baptist resources or from anyone else except the Ottawa Indians through sales of their lands. Hoag thought this lack of record keeping was at best questionable, since the Indians had given one-fourth of their property for the education of their children. Atkinson said that when he had arrived in Kansas in 1868, the Ottawas were so upset by Hutchinson and Kalloch that the Indian trustees had refused at first to meet with the board at Kalloch's house.[5]

Superintendent Hoag concluded that considerable license had been taken with the treaty provisions in this scheme and that therefore considerable damage had been done to the Ottawas. He had read the treaty of 1862 very carefully and found that it clearly outlined the powers and obligations of the school trustees—powers and obligations beyond which they could not step without a violation of their trust. Yet they had done so, particularly in fostering an institution that was to a considerable extent opposite to the real needs of the Ottawa tribe. In Hoag's view the maverick board formed in 1869 had as much right to represent the Ottawas' interests as did the original one. The federal government, he said, had been far "too tardy" in addressing these wrongs, and the time had come to restore to the Indians the property of which they had been so fraudulently deprived, before removal cut them off from it forever. It was not right to use the complications of the land situation as a blind behind which to pursue self-interest. And it was worse to claim that the guiding hand of Providence was leading in ways little understood by ordinary men.[6]

When the investigative bureaucracy of the government was enmeshed with the promotional bureaucracy of the university and the tribal bureaucracy of the Ottawas, the possible combinations among the factions became so numerous and complex that Washington officialdom was frustrated in the extreme. For example, it was feared that, if money were accepted from the old Board of Trustees for the indiscretions of Kalloch, the action would amount to a recognition of that board's legitimacy and therefore of its position against selling the school for the benefit of the Indians. Meanwhile, Atkinson and Jones were writing to Hoag complaining that the receipt given to Hutchinson did not represent the will of the tribe and should be disallowed. Other Ottawas replied that Atkinson and Jones were their enemies and were trying to destroy the tribe. Even within the anti-Atkinson group, who by 1869 were living upon the reserve in Indian Territory, there were divisions. Some wrote to the Indian Office that their chief was involved in a land speculation in Canada and was trying to persuade the council to sell both the Franklin County property in Kansas and that in the Indian Territory so that the tribe might join other Ottawas near Walpole Island in Canada.

Meanwhile, the Atkinson group in Ottawa continued to promote their various enterprises. Circulars were sent out advertising the town's new $15,000 suspension bridge, $40,000 hotel, $22,000 county building, two dentists, and ten lawyers, not to mention the $50,000 university. It was reported that since the Hoag investigation had started, Atkinson had stepped up efforts to sell lands; and the attorney for the new board, Blacklidge, was placing ads in the Ottawa papers warning purchasers that their title might not be good. The Reverend Atkinson had purchased a twenty-acre plot between the college and the town to prevent liquor dealers from compromising morality in and around the university. He intimated to Hoag that he regarded the university as a property to some extent distinct from the Indian interest. "I deny any rights of the Indians in my affairs," he said. "I have only to deal with the trustees and the government. . . . I think there are some vested rights of the University separate from the Indians."

Hoag, supposedly the disinterested investigator, was castigated by the Indian Office, after his investigation was over, for having used the proxy he held on behalf of the secretary of the interior in an attempt to sabotage the old board. E. S. Emory was president of the board and a man experienced in university squabbles, since he had represented Lawrence in a legislative fight with Emporia over the location of the University of Kansas. He complained about Hoag's active sympathy with Hutchinson and with the maverick board. Emory even went so far as to claim that Hoag had set up a school among the Ottawas to compete with the university, and that Hoag had admitted this, saying that he could not stand actions in violation of the clear intent of the treaty of 1862. Secretary Cox, whose proxy was being used, saw it less charitably. He wrote Hoag: "I am compelled to think . . . that you have been overreached in this matter, and, while I have not the slightest doubt of the honesty of your purpose, and of your effort to do what you believed was right, I am exceedingly chagrined that under the authority of my own proxy, acts should be done, which would be in the most manifest violation of the course which I have promised Mr. Emory and Mr. Atkinson I would take." Cox himself was under pressure from Hutchinson to "sift the matter to the bottom" and was warned by the former agent that a decision against him was a decision against the government and against the Indians. Of all the possibilities, however, none would suggest that the investigators were neutral, nor that any of the principals had the interest of the Indians, unmixed with other concerns, in mind.[7]

The tribe, now isolated in the Indian Territory, mourned the death of John Wilson, who had died in April, 1870, while on the way south from Kansas with his family. Wilson had contracted a fever while searching for a horse that had strayed from his camp. But those who knew him well suggested that he was also a broken-hearted man. He had always disliked the Franklin County educational scheme and, until he directed the building of an Ottawa school in Indian Territory, was often charged with being anti-education. On his last trip the fifty-five-year-old former chief had followed his displaced people, repeating, "I don't want to go. I don't want to go." Even the *Ottawa Journal,* successor to Kalloch's sheet, could, now that the situation was irreversible, compose a sympathetic postmortem upon Ottawa sovereignty in Kansas:

> When we have gotten all the rich lands of the red man, and driven the ragged unresisting remnant into the barren wilds, avarice and selfishness having nothing more to feed on, we will think romantically and kindly of the Indian and his many noble qualities, and the future boy and girl will read with tearful eyes pathetic relations of the daring, hardy, simple minded child of the forest, who trusted and was deceived as often as a maid e'er trusted her lover; and who, like woman, is just what man, the white man, has made him.[8]

Hoag's apparent sympathy with Hutchinson, which prompted him to interpret the testimony he heard in the agent's favor, affected the case against Hutchinson in the United States District Court, determining the direction of a possible final legal solution to the Ottawa problem. Hoag wrote to E. S. Parker, the United States Indian commissioner, in January, 1870, that his investigations prompted him to believe that the Indian Office should accept the receipt Hutchinson offered, as well as his argument that the missing money was not used for his own benefit. In fact, the testimony taken by Hoag at his office had turned not at all upon the legitimacy of the receipt, though it is apparent that Indian Office doubts about accepting it had justified the hearings in the first place. Hoag himself admitted that the testimony germane to this specific question "[was] so interwoven with that of the general matters of the Ottawa Indians" that without his guidance it might have been impossible to arrive at a conclusion from the original transcript.

Hoag also contended that much of the information upon which he based his antifraud conclusion involving the infamous receipt came from informal interviews with the signers of that document, that is, from persons not under oath. Actually, as was shown in depositions taken in 1879, long after the case was settled out of court to Hutchinson's advantage, Hoag had been in attendance at the meeting of the tribe at which time the receipt for the $41,993.71 was given to Hutchinson. At that time he had used his influence as superintendent of the Central Superintendency to plead with the Ottawas that Hutchinson be treated with greater compassion. On that occasion he did not argue that Hutchinson was innocent of fraudulent use of their money, but rather that the tribe stood a better chance of collecting from the United States than from Hutchinson and their only alternative was to abandon the latter tactic in order to concentrate upon the former. He told them that the Ottawas had two strings in their bow; if they let one go, they would still have the other. A question from the crowd about why Hoag was so interested in getting Hutchinson off the legal hook went unanswered, and the receipt was summarily signed. Hoag confessed to Parker in his 1870 letter that Hutchinson had been extravagant in his expenditures and "loose and unguarded in the management of his business," but he dared say nothing that would cost C. C. hard cash in the court case, fearful perhaps that his own nefarious role would be revealed. Hutchinson had voluntarily raised his bond from $10,000 to $20,000 to protect the Indians, and Hoag thought that much of his trouble could be attributed to nothing more sinister than "the influences surrounding him, his confiding nature, and the very strong assurances of liberal aid from friends East." Hoag therefore advised that the court case be dropped and that the receipt be accepted. After two more years of legal wrangling, this was exactly what happened.[9]

The Ottawa Indians, most of whom were United States

citizens by 1870, still looked to the Indian Office for protection in their land dealings. They were understandably upset that Hutchinson had sold all the timber lands in the school tract in order to support sales of trust lands. Ottawa Jones wrote Secretary Cox in June that the tribe's "credulity" in trusting Kalloch and Hutchinson had been a bad thing. He thought that the tribe's sense of discretion had declined since 1862: "They have become very trifling in every sense of the word. The very best of them are going to 'the dogs.'" Hoag would not accept the argument that Indian acquiescence in the composition of the University Board necessarily meant it was legally constituted, for the reason that the Indians had been ignorant of their rights under the treaty. This statement might as well have been applied to the receipt given to Hutchinson, though Hoag, obviously for personal reasons, defended the receipt in the manner to which he had become accustomed. The Presbyterians were interested in buying Ottawa University if it was to be sold, and the Baptists braced to defend their by-now-elaborate site, which included a nursery with 90,000 apple trees of seventy-two varieties and over 2 million Osage Orange saplings, which were to be used as hedge to fence the thriving farms of the whites in Franklin County.[10]

In 1870 a battle of legal briefs raged in Washington between Henry Beard, the attorney for the Atkinson board, and C. N. Blacklidge representing the tribe and the maverick board. Beard was particularly critical of Hoag's recommendation that the university buildings be sold and that the proceeds be given to the Indians before their removal. There was no law authorizing this, and to do it as an administrative action, Beard insisted, would be an unwarranted interference by the executive branch of government. Such actions would require the negotiation of a new treaty, and in fact representatives of the Ottawas were then in Washington attempting to do just that. Beard, in interpreting the documents connected with the affair, concluded that the Ottawas had endowed the school and that it should continue, no matter where they moved:

No more noble monument of the tribe could have been designed! Though all the present members might become citizens of the United States, and their tribal blood be imperceptibly absorbed and lost in the inevitable commingling of races, here there shall stand a living and life-giving memorial of the spirit and character of the chiefs, councillors, and people of the tribe who directed and controlled it in the year 1862.

Beard wrote that Blacklidge would make a $10,000 fee if he won the case for the Indians, and that Hutchinson's attorney, Wilson Shannon, also on the new board, was of the opinion that he could get *U.S. v. C. C. Hutchinson* dismissed if the old board were found to have been illegally constituted. To Beard it was apparent that the grand scheme was continuing in the manipulations of the new board, which paid little attention to the education of Indians and a great deal to the interest of its principals. The schemers were attempting to saddle the university with Hutchinson's $41,993.73 debt to the government by promising the Indians that the sale of the university would yield bigger profits than the pursuit of Hutchinson. In Beard's view,

> This transaction of the new board demands a note of admiration, as being one of the most remarkable schemes for Indian education ever brought to public notice. The combination of speculators in 1864 to swing a large University in aid of a town-site speculation is insignificant in contrast with this combination of Hutchinson's attorneys in the matter of applying the educational funds of the Ottawa University to pay Hutchinson's liabilities to the United States.

The Indians, contended Beard, had been perfectly satisfied with the university, even though it had been erected by defrauding them, until certain lawyers corrupted greedy tribal factions into calculating, on the model of the white squatters, the exact cash value of their chance at civilization.[11]

Blacklidge responded in August, 1870. He pointed to

the strange composition of the original board and its eager-
ness to sell the first 5,000 acres to John Young, Hutchinson's father-in-law. The board had traveled 1,500 miles to
do that, and that had been its only action in two years.
Hutchinson's influence could be seen there and in nearly
every action of the board later on. But he was not alone in
his chicanery. The agent "virtually controlled and moulded
[sic] the actions of that body to suit his own conveniences,
pleasure and interest, or the interests of those he represented, by whom *he* was used as a cat's paw to manipu-
late and deceive these poor Indians, and do the dirty work
of these 'professed Christians' who also induced him to use
a large amount of money [i.e., proceeds of sales of trust
lands] that did not belong to him, or them, thereby involving him in utter ruin, pecuniarily." Blacklidge contended
that the power of this "Christian Ring" was so great that
outside offers of up to $2.50 an acre for the original lands
had been refused in order to give the ring's members an
inside deal. The records of Franklin County confirm that
the first 5,000 acres were divided by Young among distinguished individuals and thus used to maximum advantage. When that was done, the board had proceeded to
build a magnificent school, though there were only thirty
Ottawa children of school age, and there was no authorization to spend more than the proceeds of the 5,000
acres, which had been sold for a mere pittance. Blacklidge went to great lengths to describe the "extravagent
and unknown costs" of the university building. It was "fin-
ished with select and learned professors, representing almost all the modern sciences, adorned with mahogany and
rosewood pianos, presided over by worthy descendants of
'Beethoven,' and all this at the expense of the defenseless
Indians."

At the time of reckoning when Atkinson arrived in 1868,
Kalloch had been freed from his obligations for illegal
sales, and Hutchinson had become the scapegoat, though
not for the full amount of his sales, for those lands that he
had sold for less than their appraised value. It was found

that he had made sales at an average of $7.00 an acre, which in the "unselfishly Christian judgement" of the board was not enough, though it had previously sold the best lands to Young for $1.25. The board did not allow Hutchinson's expenses to be applied against the debt as it had with Kalloch, presumably because Hutchinson had by that time fallen from grace in the eyes of the Baptists.

All the Baptist talk of the wonderful things missionary Jotham Meeker had done for the Ottawas in the 1850s could not, wrote Blacklidge, disguise the essentially selfish nature of the university scheme. The goal of the "Christian Ring" since 1858 had been land speculation. Its objective was to pocket the proceeds and continue the school for Indians only so long as formal tribal relations with the government were legally intact. It made sure in the treaty of 1862 that these tribal relations would pass out of existence in a few years. Still, to deny, as the board had done and still did, that the Indians had the right to inquire into the disposition of funds connected with the university required, according to Blacklidge, "a degree of sublime impudence, rarely attained."[12]

In the spring of 1871, Beard responded for the trustees with still another printed brief. The Ottawas, he said, only enjoyed the right to send their children to the university, where they would be clothed and fed, and could claim no other rights whatsoever in relation to the school. The board regretted, continued Beard, that the Ottawas had removed from Kansas and were largely unable to avail themselves of this privilege of attendance, but the removal was in no way the responsibility of the University Board. The Atkinson group had made plans to establish some sort of school for Ottawa children in the Indian Territory, but it was in no way obligated by any treaty to do so. The Indians would simply have to get rid of the "impracticable notion" that they had some right of property in the university buildings and land. The delegation of Indians that had visited Washington in 1869 to try to get a treaty turning the university over to the tribe was, according to Beard, off on a "preposterous" mission. James Wind and William Hurr were on the Board of Trustees; they not only knew what was going on but also in fact had participated in the settlement. Beard said that Wind and Hurr had had full knowledge of the sale of the first 5,000 acres to Young and in 1864 had themselves requested that the secretary of the interior issue patents to him. An 1866 letter from Wind, Hurr, and other Ottawas indicated they knew the trust lands were nearly all sold and that timber land from the university tract was being conveyed with trust lands. That letter reportedly said that the tribe wanted the university built and requested that the remaining trust lands be sold in order to do it. In 1867 there was, continued Beard, a letter from Wind and Hurr saying that the last 7,000 acres of trust lands should be sold to the university trustees. The lands that were now proposed to be returned to the Ottawas included the entire townsite of Ottawa and many farms. Beard concluded, "The proposition that the United States shall seize and attempt to sell the lands held by the University, would not only ruin its present prospects, but create general distrust and dissatisfaction."[13]

The letters mentioned by Beard are preserved in government files relating to Ottawa University. The tone of them, however, is subject to a different interpretation. For example, the April, 1866, series reveals that Hutchinson took the first initiative in advising that the remainder of the trust lands be sold to the university. The approval by a faction of the tribe was only implied: "We want to become citizens as soon as practicable, and to have authority to sell any and all of our lands," they wrote. It is evident that at that point those tribal members knew about the trust-land and timber sales, but there is no indication that they did in fact approve of them. The letter from Wind, Hurr, and others of April 2, 1866, stated that "our agent" had sold nearly all the trust lands and that "the college trustees" had been adding timber lands to those transactions. The letter did *not* say that this was justifiable in order to build the university, but rather noted that all this had been done and still the university had not been built. The letter requested permission from the Indian Office for Hutchinson to go east to raise funds to build the college that had been promised but not provided despite the substantial reduction of the tribal domain.

In his 1866 correspondence Hutchinson was embarrassed at the revelation that trust lands had been sold. He wrote Superintendent Thomas Murphy in January of that year that he had never recognized or encouraged any sales of trust lands and had always warned whites against purchase. The timber sales, he said, were carried out at the request of the Indians and because the agent thought it would be for their benefit. There is every evidence that that explanation was contrived and an outright fraud. In February, 1864, Hutchinson had written John Pratt that he had selected 1,500 acres of school land, not among the 5,000 acres reserved for the university, as timber land, and that the 1,500 acres had to be sold that spring at $8.00 to $10.00 an acre to settlers. He did not then consider the land "worthless prairie," but on the contrary stated, "This will give us a fund to use." Certainly Hutchinson's approach in an 1870 article on the benefits of immigration was not reticent. Whoever comes to Franklin County to profit himself, he wrote, will profit the whole community. By 1872 the former Ottawa agent had laid out a new town along the Santa Fe railroad at its crossing of the Big Arkansas River. This city, originally designed as a haven for prohibition-minded people, to this day bears the name of a man who was nothing if not a promoter of economic development—Hutchinson, Kansas.[14]

Those investigating the matter were not convinced by Beard's arguments. Hutchinson, struggling in court for what remained of his fortune, turned upon Atkinson and the Baptists. He testified that Atkinson had furnished and occupied rooms for his personal use in the university building before school rooms were made available to the Indians, and that the original plan was modified in order to convert rooms intended for children into a palatial residence for the representative of the Home Mission Board. There was the odd fact that only one Ottawa Indian child was attending the "Indian school" at Ottawa in 1871— Idelette Jones, the daughter of John T. Jones.

The *New York Times* in the summer of that year published letters indicating that the Interior Department was not satisfied with the defense of the Atkinson board. Too little was known, thought the department, of the early history of the university, though the official records in its possession in Washington showed "a clear case of fraud in the early transactions with the Indians." Atkinson responded sharply in a letter to the *Times* denying that the Baptist involvement with the tribe had been a "plundering expedition" and again affirmed that the tribe was pleased with the actions taken. The local Ottawa paper expressed the hope that this defense would end the long investigation, as well as attempts by a ring to crush the city's major improvement. In the same issue the town congratulated itself on having been chosen the site for major maintenance shops of the Leavenworth, Lawrence, and Galveston Railroad.[15]

The year 1872 was the most crucial in a parade of tense years for the Ottawa schemers. Hutchinson, who by then was also being sued by Samuel Levy of New York for defaulting on a promissory note, moved to settle the federal embezzlement case. It would seem that an out-of-court compromise, given the earlier suspicions of prosecuting attorney Albert Horton regarding his predecessor and the hold placed on Hutchinson's real estate, would have been quite impossible, and that the case would definitely be tried to a decision. Interior Secretary J. D. Cox had written Judge Horton when the attorney was put on the case in 1869 that "no arrangement or compromise of any sort has been contemplated or will be allowed." In the fall of 1870, Horton had Hutchinson arrested because the defendant was delaying the hearings by failing to appear. He reaffirmed his determination to obtain a decision and thus calm the controversy by taking it out of the political forum. Yet late in December, 1871, Hutchinson made a compromise offer, and Horton accepted it in mid-January, 1872. Hutchinson pleaded innocent, but agreed to reimburse the government in part for the expenses of its investigation, promising to pay the United States Treasury $1,000. Horton, who had started out the reformer, now held that "in view of all the circumstances of the case" —that Hutchinson's bond was only $20,000, that the Ottawas had given him a receipt, and that Hoag had recommended accepting the receipt—that perhaps it would be best to abandon the effort to corner Hutchinson and to accept the $1,000 out-of-court settlement. The indiscretions of the former district attorney Riggs doubtlessly were also on Horton's mind, and he surely perceived the technical difficulties regarding the strict legality of his own motion for retrial in 1869. The Interior Department issued a curt approval of this proposal, and the case was closed in February, 1872.[16]

The more the historian examines this series of actions, the more questionable the whole picture becomes. Horton, despite his initial reforming zeal, was an old friend of both Atkinson and Kalloch, having served with the latter as an elector for Ulysses S. Grant in 1868 and on numerous boards before that. In 1884, long after the apparent settlement of the Ottawa scheme, Horton had occasion to remember it again, when he was chief justice of the Kansas Supreme Court, having followed the usual successful political career. Perhaps for some legal reason, or out of political conscience, he requested that the Treasury Department send him copies of all the papers relating to the Hutchinson trial and his role in it. His recollection of it was surprisingly vague, considering that it had been his first case as district attorney, and considering its bizarre nature, even for the Gilded Age. In his letter to the United States attorney general requesting the documents, he claimed he had "prosecuted the case to a final judgement, but that afterwards some compromise or settlement was made at Washington with C. C. Hutchinson and I received letters, as I remember, from your Department requesting me to take no further action in the premises." To the solicitor of the Treasury he wrote a similar letter, specifically stating that he had obtained a judgment for $20,000, the amount of Hutchinson's bond, against the former agent. No such judgment was ever recorded by the court and no evidence of pressure from Washington offices has been preserved in the National Archives. There does remain Horton's letter of January, 1872, in which he recommended the $1,000 settlement and for very certain reasons. It could well be that political pressure in 1884 made it expedient for Horton to forget the critical role that he had played in the Hutchinson case. What effect the infinite imagination and legal tactics of Hutchinson had upon Horton in 1872, and what promises may have been exchanged concerning the future, can only be surmised. The certain thing is that the Ottawa Indians again played odd man out in C. C. Hutchinson's game of changing partners.[17]

The Indian Office was never satisfied with this method of relieving Hutchinson of his obligations to that department. As late as 1876, amid frantic preparations for centennial exhibits, Indian Commissioner J. Q. Smith inquired why the infamous receipt had been accepted and the $1,000 settlement made. Smith insisted that an exhaustive search of Indian Office records had failed to demonstrate that the commissioner had ever been consulted about the compromise, even though Hutchinson as an official agent was under his jurisdiction, as were the Ottawa trust funds, which remained short the sum of $41,993.73. Wrote Smith:

As a question of settlement with the Indians, I am obliged to conclude that the acceptance of such a prayer [the receipt] as a valid voucher in the hands of an agent of the United States would be every way contrary both to the laws for settlement and disbursement of moneys put into the hands of an agent, or coming into them by authority of law and would also be contrary to every sound rule of policy in regard to the dealings of agents with Indian tribes, opening the door to so great abuses as to make it impossible for the Department to accept such a mode of settlement.

Smith was not even able to determine whether the secretary of the interior had provided his official consent. The critical letter, however, exists, indicating that Secretary of the Interior Columbus Delano, then himself under considerable fire for cavorting with the Indian Ring, had bypassed the then commissioner of Indian affairs, Seneca Indian Ely Parker, to approve quietly a settlement that was never recognized by the office directly responsible. It was perhaps Hutchinson's finest, most sinister coup.[18]

8

Victory and Defeat

THE LIABILITIES of Ottawa University remained unresolved. On June 29, 1872, Congress dealt the Atkinson board its most crushing blow to date by passing Senate Bill No. 1172, "For the Relief of Certain Indians of the Central Superintendency." J. P. C. Shanks, head of the House Committee on Indian Affairs, took the occasion of the debate on this bill to "fire a bombshell," emphasizing that the University Board had withheld the names of the purchasers of land, many of whom were men with political influence who may have been given privileged information in return for support. That revelation insured passage of the bill, and Atkinson's opposition was branded as "mere pretense."

Bill No. 1172 provided that a commission of three should be appointed to investigate carefully once again the affairs of Ottawa University, to appraise its property, and to take possession of the school. The entire plant was then to be sold, and the proceeds distributed to the Ottawas, whose former domain had been the origin of the whole enterprise. The Congress was especially moved by a petition from the Ottawas saying that white men had taken control of the school lands in a manner not authorized by treaty, and that they seemed accountable to no one in the executive bureaucracy: "We totally and wholly repudiate and

146

protest against the claim of any parties to dictate to us what shall be done with our school property, simply because they have possession of it." The tribe offered to refund any money contributed by the Baptists, but emphasized its determination to realize its fair share of the university's value. Attorney Henry Beard, for the University Board, responded with the charge that the memorial bore "internal evidence of being the work of other persons than those who have signed it."[1]

The response from the board and the Baptists to the appointment of the commission headed by soon-to-be President James A. Garfield was immediate, loud, and desperate. Government officials began sending letters to one another, decrying with incredulity the strong objections to a bill they believed was fair under the circumstances. Before passage Atkinson had written the Honorable J. M. Williams, a Baptist, that the "vile bill" was the work of the Indian Ring. Edward Tobey of the Board of Indian Commissioners admitted immediately after passage that pressure upon him from "prominent friends of Ottawa University" in Boston had been great, and that Atkinson had organized a strong lobbying effort against implementation of the bill. Tobey spoke with Williams regarding the matter, and Williams in turn spoke with President Grant with the view of working out a compromise that might be satisfactory to both the Indians and the Board of Trustees. Given the impasse that had developed over the years, that was certainly impossible, and the efforts at compromise were in actuality a screen for a move to reverse the decision to confiscate and leave the situation exactly as it was. They wanted a new Kansas university and a townsite free not only of the presence of the Indians whose lands had made it possible but also of any financial obligation to the Ottawas. Roscoe Conkling, one of the most powerful men in the Senate, wrote Delano on the day of the bill's passage, requesting that it be suspended. Certain prominent Baptists were in a state of shock. One of them wrote Delano that the Home Mission Society had supported 5,500 missionaries, preached 500,000 sermons, baptized 61,000 people, and built 2,000 churches, plus at least one Indian University. "Pray for them! Help support them! Do it now! Do it for Jesus!" he exhorted.[2]

The *Ottawa Journal* was incensed that all university property, including that claimed to have been bought with donations and the 7,000 acres of trust lands purchased outright from the tribe after the 1867 treaty, was to be taken for the benefit of the "noble red man." Certainly Congress did not perceive, wrote the *Journal*, that the Ottawa University of Kansas and the Ottawa Indian school were two distinct things. To the historian Congress's perception is wholly understandable, however, since there never was any distinction included in the treaties. Isaac Kalloch, returning to the public eye for the occasion, wrote an attack on the new bill in the *Lawrence Tribune*, stating that the act had been pressed through Congress and was based upon a misunderstanding of the institution's history and intentions, as well as its vindication by previous investigators. "The Baptist communicants of this state will be heard before this outrage is consummated," threatened Kalloch.[3]

The Baptist communicants were indeed heard, all the way to the office of the president of the United States, whom they asked late in July to use his powers to override Congress in this "unusual and extraordinary case." T. C. Sears, chief attorney for the powerful Missouri Kansas and Texas railroad company wrote Interior Secretary Columbus Delano that the implementation of the act must be delayed for political reasons if for no other. If the execution of the confiscation act would lose any votes for the Republicans in the election year of 1872, which it certainly would in the East, it should be postponed at least until after the November polling. Atkinson went personally to Grant's summer house at Long Branch, New Jersey, and spoke to the president about salvaging the university in the face of this new threat.[4]

The Kansas press, responding to those actions, and by

this time calloused to the challenges of civilized enterprise by Indian rights in the state, predicted that, no matter how bleak the prospect for the Ottawa University in the summer of 1872, it doubtless would survive even this latest onslaught and perhaps even prosper from it. The *Ottawa Herald* put the situation simply: "Kalloch is a warm supporter of Grant. Grant has control over the Indian Department. The Indian Department has control over certain documents relating to misappropriations of public funds of Ottawa Indians. Kalloch was with the Ottawas. He supports Grant." That conclusion seems valid, given, for example, the attitude of Garfield, who was so busy at the time with a mission to the Flathead Indians that he made no mention at all in his voluminous diary of his appointment to the Ottawa commission. Still, the *Lawrence Tribune* had some respect for Congressman Garfield's ability to sift out the truth and thought it still possible that white Ottawa might "lose a slice of her valuable city." J. P. C. Shanks, chairman of the House Committee on Indian Affairs, was certainly determined enough. He telegraphed Delano early in August: "Do not suspend action on the Ottawa University matter. Take charge of it at once."[5]

The congressional commission went to Kansas in 1872, as its instructions required, and it presented to Atkinson an order to turn over the school property for appraisal. This the Baptist leader flatly refused to do. W. R. Irwin, who had replaced Garfield as head of the commission, had no guidelines for a response of that sort. He wrote to Commissioner of Indian Affairs F. A. Walker for further instructions. Atkinson denied the rights of the commission on grounds that the present University Board had legal title and the congressional confiscation act of June, 1872, was unconstitutional. Why specifically it was unconstitutional was not mentioned.

Rather than imprison Atkinson and the entire board, who obviously were well connected economically and politically in the East, Irwin decided to subpoena them to appear before the commission on August 19 and explain once again the events of the Ottawa intrigue. During the latter part of the month, one by one, the whole cast came trailing in—Kalloch, Emory, Atkinson, and numerous lesser lights who had been unable to trail Hutchinson out of the tangle via legal informalities. This time Atkinson appeared with a list of Baptist donors, the first concrete evidence of outside aid to the university. Nathan Bishop of the Board of Indian Commissioners had given $1,000; the First Baptist Church of Newark, New Jersey, $1,000; the Washington Avenue Church of Brooklyn, $1,000; the Tabernacle Baptist Church of New York, $1,000. There followed names of churches and individual Baptists in Chicago, Dayton, Cleveland, Pittsburgh, Philadelphia, Hartford, Boston, and numerous smaller places. Admittedly, not all the money pledged was actually paid, and the evidence of outside donations made Hutchinson's explanation of where more than $41,000 of the Ottawas' money had gone look all the more suspicious. But the ring was badly split and it attempted to confront one problem at a time.

The list of donors buttressed the Baptists' claim to some shade of title independent of the Indians, though it was never claimed that Baptist pledges amounted to more than $30,000 of the $100,000-to-$300,000 real value of the property. The commissioners, not satisfied, finished an inventory of the property, valuing the land alone at $108,000. On August 20 they approached Atkinson again about relinquishing control of the school. Reverend Atkinson was not at home: he had been "called to the country on business," but had left word that his answer was still no. Completely frustrated, the commission advised Washington that the board's determination to maintain possession of the property was likely to intensify. An impasse had been reached.

Tauy Jones had died on August 16 and left his real estate, worth over $25,000, to Ottawa University for the endowment of a school of theology, on the condition that the board or its successors should remain in control. "Ottawa Jones," who had been the principal originator of the scheme while tribe hopping in the 1850s, had in death made one of his most telling moves. In the summer of 1872 the prospect was for a long-drawn court battle like that with Hutchinson, perhaps with equally indecisive results.[6]

Late in the autumn of that year any reasonable consensus in Washington on the Ottawa question began to disintegrate, as departments were set against each other by an issue and combination of operators apparently beyond the power of any to control effectively. In October, Ottawas such as Francis King and Henry Clay wrote to the Indian Office, objecting to reports that the Hutchinson case had been dropped. These men, who later were to swear out depositions stating that Enoch Hoag had unduly influenced the tribe to grant Hutchinson a receipt, explained that they had remained silent about their interpretation of the receipt only because the Indians had been told that the attorney general of the United States had ruled the receipt should not be accepted, which, in fact, he had. Also, the dissenting Indians had been afraid that bringing up the issue of the $41,993.71 might affect tribal rights to the college property—that is, Washington might give them the money and the Baptists the university. The Indian Office inquired of the Interior Department how this tribal concern had been allowed to develop. Interior Secretary Delano meanwhile was upset with the congressional response, and on December 7 he expressed the view that the Baptists had been right in resisting the hastily passed act of June, 1872. Because of their resistance, and because the Atkinson board was making an impressive show of strength in Kansas and elsewhere, he had not advertised or sold the lands as directed by the act. He declared that he would not until more "practical" legislation on the matter had been passed. Delano believed that the treaties had plainly been violated, that the funds from the land sales had not been invested under the terms of the trust, that the management of the university had been "irregular and careless, if not improvident and wasteful,"

and that the unnecessarily large building was being run
for the benefit of whites. Still, he maintained that Congress had not provided "practical" action. Rather than institute a suit against the University Board under the June
law, as the attorney general's office had advised him, Delano asked for more legislation. Meanwhile, on the executive front President Grant, fresh from conversations at
Long Branch with Atkinson, intervened to block the course
of events. In 1899 he was credited by a local historian,
whose source of information was Atkinson a few years
later, with having "saved the school" single-handed.[7]

Meanwhile, the University Board stood united against
the divided and confused Washington bureaucracy. In its
minutes of December 28, 1872, the board passed a formal
resolution refusing to recognize the 1872 act and appointed
Henry Beard and John Pratt to act as its agents in Washington for the final struggle. It was hopeful that a new bill,
Senate Bill No. 1290, would pass. This proposal called for
some cash settlement commensurate with the Ottawas'
original contribution, while leaving the university intact
and firmly in the hands of the board. On this matter, the
guiding light of Providence seemed clear, especially in
view of the Baptists' position that "extensive and imposing
buildings have an elevating and inspiring effect upon students, professors, patrons—indeed, upon all who behold
them." No squabble should separate the Baptists from
their monument to civilized enterprise. The proceedings
of the Philadelphia Baptist Educational Convention of 1872
are particularly indicative of their philosophy:

> The Parthenon of the Greeks, the proud old baronial halls
> and feudal castes, have wrought a wonderful influence upon
> the world—have given tone to its philosophy, its poetry, elo-
> quence, science, art; have given shape and hue to its life—
> have done much to form its morals, as well as its taste; to
> fix its religion, to form and control its government—to deter-
> mine indeed the destinies of men. The Jew fought the Roman,
> while the temple stood.

Indeed, the great cut-stone pile on the prairie at Ottawa could be credited with an influence hardly less profound, though a great deal less salutory, than the convention claimed for it.[8]

On March 3, 1873, the long-sought compromise legislation was passed by white congressmen, who apparently had learned that the justice applied to the realities of Indian affairs was not as clear as it appeared in the abstract. The legislation created a new commission comprised of W. R. Irwin and S. R. Smith of the frustrated 1872 commission and Henry Neal of Ohio, A. J. Emory of Massachusetts, and professor Joseph Henry of the Smithsonian Institution. It included as many distinguished names as the first commission had, but its charge was not nearly so formidable. Rather than demand that the university and its lands be sold for the Ottawas' benefit, the new commission was instructed to negotiate with the Ottawas, the Baptist Home Mission Society, and the university trustees and to sanction any settlement that might be reasonably determined. In effect, Congress had capitulated. Rather than make a decision in a matter in which so many people and groups had failed, Congress opted for the pattern that had been established by the district attorneys, lawyers, and departmental officials and, weary of the case, left the Ottawas to be introduced to the world of citizenship by those with more experience in such matters.[9]

S. S. Cutting of the Baptist Home Mission Board grasped the spirit and essence of the new proposal almost immediately. He wrote to Secretary Delano, asking that the Baptists be allowed to appoint two men to vote Delano's proxy in the matter, so that none could say the denomination was damaged from the outside. This was granted. Meanwhile, meetings under the new arrangement proceeded with caution. The Ottawas reported that, though the university property had been appraised by the 1872 commission at $108,000, the Baptists were offering only $40,000 in settlement. The University Board acted independently of the Baptists and more definitely. It claimed that the Ottawa tribe had ceased to exist when all Ottawas became citizens in 1869 under the terms of the 1867 treaty, and that therefore the Indians had no claim to anything from them or the Baptists. It observed that these Indians, when they had come to Kansas from Ohio, had been "uncivilized and idolatrous savages." Now seven-eighths of the Ottawas were Baptists, and they had subsidized a $50,000 building, from which their children did not benefit; had lost 74,000 acres of land; and were living in poverty in Indian Territory surrounded by hostile tribes. Thus they had reaped the benefits of "civilization." The Home Mission Society, the Ottawas, and the commission came to an agreement in July to give to the university the building and 640 acres of land and to sell the remaining land for the benefit of the Ottawas. The University Board, however, curtly refused to accept that agreement and hired attorneys to represent it at a meeting of the commission in Boston.[10]

In October an agreement was reached that seemed fair to all parties, except the Indians. The University Board was the principal benefactor. The school received, in addition to the 640-acre farm directly adjacent to the building, 1,280 acres of the unsold portion of the school lands set apart in 1862. The board and the Home Mission Society were left to their own devices to agree upon a division of this between themselves. The Indians were to receive for their educational fund the interest on 50 percent of the proceeds from the sale of the remaining lands after deduction of attorneys' fees and discounts on notes and mortgages. After five years one-third of the principal of this fund would go to the tribe per capita; after ten years, one-half; and after fifteen years, the remainder. Thus a great deal was left to the discretion of the trustees to be appointed for the sale of the remaining lands, as well as the U.S. District Court for the Southern District of Kansas, which was responsible for determining the attorneys' fees on behalf of the Ottawas. Just prior to this compromise agreement of October 29, 1873, Enoch Hoag wrote to Secretary Delano that it was "not . . . equitable to the Indians, but . . . equity cannot be reached." Hoag objected to the university receiving 1,280 acres more land than it had been authorized to hold by treaty, after the possibilities of those covenants had been stretched to the absolute limit. But Hoag was tired also. "Believing this is the most that can be made for the interest of the Indians . . . ," he wrote, "and to avoid any further litigation in the case . . . I recommend approval."[11]

The Home Mission Board was the first to learn who in the final, flexible settlement was to "make the most of it." The university trustees, who had argued for years that they claimed the land because of contributions from the Home Mission Society, now refused the recognize that the society had made any contributions or to reward it with a share of the lands. Through the year 1874 the university trustees and the board of the Home Mission Society argued about what would be "an equitable part" of the 1,280 acres to give to the mission group on behalf of Meeker's long labors among the Ottawas and the alleged support from the East during the school's crisis in the sixties. The university trustees thought a fair settlement was no settlement at all and refused to answer the letters of the Home Mission Board. The Baptists had extracted, in joint meetings with the commission, the promise from the university trustees that in return for the patent on the 640 acres on which the building stood, the building would always be devoted to educational purposes under the auspices of the Baptist denomination, which it has been to this day. S. S. Cutting's claim for $3,835.77 in cash or land for "services" and attorneys' fees was judged by the school trustees "exorbitant and unjust." The university trustees were prevented by the 1873 agreement from ever mortgaging the 640 acres, and so they were depending on mortgages on the whole 1,280 acres to pay the debts of the extended litigation. Also, grants of lands in the tract were being made to attorneys whom the trustees owed, and to Rev. R. Atkinson as well, who asserted that his services were worth no less than a grant of 320 acres. Finally, in 1876 the Home Mission Board managed to obtain 160 acres from the trustees. At the same time they demanded a patent in their own name, because they felt that a university involved in so many law suits could not pass a good title. Even then the university trustees held that the Mission Society should not be so greedy, since it was rich while the university was poor.[12]

The Ottawas of Blanchard's Fork and Roche de Boeuf enjoyed no such benefits. A commission consisting of Enoch Hoag, George Barker, and Washington Hadley sold the remaining Ottawa lands in Kansas, roughly 10,000 acres of the original 74,000. By 1878 attorneys for the tribe estimated that, though the sum of $50,000 had been realized from these sales, the Indians had received a miserly total of $260. The tribe claimed it was "being robbed by the trustees" and repeatedly asked for an annual accounting of where the tribe stood financially. The three trustees, however, not only made no account to the Ottawas but also made only one report, in 1875, to the judge of the District Court of Kansas, to whom by the terms of the 1873 agreement they were to report annually. That one report of sales was never audited, and attorneys for the tribe were certain that it was incorrect. The trustees for the lands were also required to report each July 1 to the secretary of the interior, but they made no reports to that officer in the years before 1878, though they claimed to have sold nearly all the land. Perhaps this could be forgiven as a typical bureaucratic bungle, but the Ottawas did not think so. Their lawyers charged that a "ring" at Lawrence was operating in conjunction with the trustees. When one of the Lawrence ring found a buyer for Ottawa land, a double transfer would be made. The trustees would sell it to the ring member at a lower figure and then divide the money gained from the resale. Only upon the original sale was accounting to the Ottawas required. In one case, according to tribal attorneys, McMillan, a member of the ring, sold on August 28, 1876, 602 acres for

$4,800. On October 10 the trustees conveyed this officially to McMillan for $977 to pass on to his client, leaving a profit of $3,823 to divide among the inside group. Obviously, it was an advantage to delay any careful audit until these jugglings ceased.[13]

What money was eventually paid to the Ottawas was diminished by attorney's fees. Attorneys had found Indian Office business lucrative for years, and it was the practice to charge the Indians through their trust funds 40 percent or more of any amount recovered for them by the legal profession. Since they were helpless to recover anything at all without the aid of white attorneys, they had no practical option but to agree. Enoch Hoag was especially disturbed about this practice in the case of the Ottawas, whom he felt had been more exploited than most tribes.

Hoag had insisted, when the October, 1873, compromise was made, that if he were to serve with the trustees for the sale, the Ottawa attorneys must reduce their claim for fees from $20,000 to $16,000 and accept certain notes held by the Ottawas at a reasonable discount. Hoag had also asked to be present when the judge awarded the attorneys' fees. When this was done in 1878, however, Hoag was not notified, and the attorneys, who then were charging Hoag himself with fraud in the land sales, convinced the judge to give them $20,000 and to value the interest-paying notes at only 70 percent of their face value. Hoag had predicted this, knowing that, when it came time for payment, "the attorneys for the Indians would not be unmindful before the judge of their own interests . . . I believe the time had passed in which the rights and interest of the Indians would be protected under their contract with them." Hoag's one trump card had been that, if the attorneys did not play the fee question his way, he would "lay the whole matter before the department." What additional indiscretions he knew of will never be known. Perhaps because of fear of retaliation and his own vulnerability to counter charges, Hoag did nothing more than express disgust at the conduct of the Ottawa attorneys, who went so far as to submit charges for a man who had never been authorized to act for the tribe. As late as 1882 the struggle was still going on. The Ottawa attorneys then asked the U.S. District Court to investigate the accounts of the trustees for the sale, saying that "an honest investigation of the receipts and expenditures will open the eyes of the incredulous." Nothing of substance resulted.[14]

The aftermath of the grand scheme was pitiful. John Earley, newly designated Ottawa chief, and other former Ottawa Indians, now citizens, petitioned the District Court in 1883 to dismiss the three land trustees, who were drawing a salary of $500 a year from the funds reserved for them. They insisted that many former Ottawas were thrifty and some were possessors of considerable wealth, and that they were competent to invest the money still in the hands of the trustees. They insisted that the trust be dissolved and the money distributed. At a final hearing that spring the three trustees' attorneys objected to the appearance of a government attorney to oversee the final settlement, arguing, as had the University Board before them, that the Ottawas did not exist as a tribe and therefore, the federal government had no right to interfere on their behalf. The court concluded the matter with the determination that the trustees had in notes and money a sum of $7,280.88 — all that was left of the once-magnificent 74,000-acre Ottawa domain. In 1902, J. W. McGowan, a Washington, D.C., attorney, inquired of the General Land Office concerning what he believed to be a fraudulent receipt granted to an agent named Hutchinson in the 1870s. He wondered why the Ottawas had never been paid the nearly $42,000 involved. His reasonable inquiry was ignored.[15]

In 1875 a fire broke out in the impressive building at Ottawa University known as Tauy Jones Hall. It completely gutted the structure and destroyed its ornate mahogany woodwork. The people of Ottawa dutifully pitched in to repair and reroof the building, well knowing how much it had meant to them in their invasion of Franklin County. By then the last Ottawas on the University Board, Wind and Hurr, had resigned, and Isaac Kalloch was back in the pulpit, where he had started in the 1850s. In February, 1874, he held forth before his congregation at the First Baptist Church in Ottawa and insisted that the sanctuary was his true home. There he had chosen to be rather than to accept a call to the United States Senate. He was glad —glad to be back in the pulpit after a ten-year interruption, including the Ottawa speculation and other town ventures—glad for this respite in the Lord's house of the small town that he had help make before going on to political success and then failure as mayor of San Francisco. He took as his text Isaiah 2:3:

> And many people shall go and say, Come ye, and let us go up to the mountain of the LORD, to the house of the God of Jacob; and he will teach us of his ways, and we will walk in his paths: for out of Zion shall go forth the law, and the word of the LORD from Jerusalem.[16]

9

Legal Atonement

WHILE the various investigations ran their dreary course in Washington and Kansas, the Ottawas attempted to establish a new life on the 12,000-acre reservation they had purchased from the Shawnees. Located in the extreme northeastern corner of the Indian Territory between Spring River on the east and the Neosho River on the west, the land was well watered and no less timbered and fertile than their lands in Kansas. In fact, the majority of the Ottawas resented their new location much less than the move itself and their unilateral dispossession in Kansas. By the mid-1880s many of the small but potentially productive Ottawa farms were the envy of outsiders, especially those whites who hoped for a blanket allotment policy, the destruction of tribal cohesion and common land ownership, and eventual statehood for the Indian Territory.

The forces leading to the formal dissolution of the Ottawa tribe dated back to the treaties of the 1860s. Article One of the 1862 treaty held that,

> The Ottawa Indians of the united bands of Blanchard's Fork and of Roche de Boeuf, having become sufficiently advanced in civilization, and being desirous of becoming citizens of the United States, it is hereby agreed and stipulated that their organization, and their relations with the United States as an

Indian tribe shall be dissolved and terminated at the expiration of five years from the ratification of this treaty; and from and after that time the said Ottawas, and each and every one of them, shall be deemed and declared to be citizens of the United States.[1]

The treaty of 1867 deferred citizenship to July 16, 1869, though heads of individual Ottawa families could go before the United States District Court of Kansas and secure earlier citizenship for themselves and their immediate families. In so doing, they relinquished tribal affiliation and membership and were entitled to their share of whatever tribal funds were available at the time. The 1867 treaty also provided immediate patents for the Kansas allotments granted in 1862, so that the sale of those plots could be expedited and the removal to Indian Territory accomplished with greater dispatch. As a gesture toward native authority, cases of disputed heirship were to be adjudicated by tribal officials, not the United States.[2]

The bulk of the Kansas allotments were sold almost immediately, and the majority of the tribe made the move to Indian Territory in the years 1868 and 1869. Even though the distance was not excessive, too much loose cash, general malnutrition, the pressure of past debts and of the ever-present whiskey merchants, and ineptitude in the operation of the Spring River branch of the Neosho Agency took a heavy toll in Ottawa life. According to Joseph B. King, who served as "Assistant Chief" for the advance guard of emigrants, nearly half of the tribe died within a short time after their arrival in Indian Territory. Additional problems were created with the construction of the Atlantic and Pacific Railroad from Seneca, Missouri, to Vinita, Indian Territory, in the summer and fall of 1871. Cutting across the Quapaw lands just south of the Ottawas, the railroad attracted a horde of construction workers, livestock merchants, land speculators, whiskey merchants, gamblers, and prostitutes. One newspaper reported, perhaps with some exaggeration, that in Vinita—less than twenty miles

from the Ottawa reservation—the only respectable inhabitants were United States marshals attempting to regulate
the houses of prostitution. It was little wonder then that
in the closing months of 1871, Central Superintendent
Enoch Hoag was informed that the Ottawas and their Indian neighbors were experiencing "a deep feeling of insecurity."[3]

This insecurity intensified with passage of the General
Allotment (or Dawes) Act of 1887. By then many of the
Ottawas had achieved citizenship and had fared reasonably
well in the adjustment to agrarian life along the Neosho.
But unlike the Five Civilized Tribes and the neighboring
Miamis, Senecas, and Peorias, the Ottawas were not specifically excluded from the provisions of the Act of 1887.
They did, however, hold off federal agents until the early
1890s, when additional legislation made allotment a fore-
gone conclusion. The first of these was the act of February
28, 1891, an amendment to the 1887 legislation, commonly
known as the Agricultural or Grazing Leasing Act. Its
essential stipulation was that the president of the United
States was empowered to allot in eighty-acre plots those
Indian reservations that were "advantageous for agricultural or grazing purposes." If it was determined by the
secretary of the interior that an individual allottee could
not personally and with benefit to himself occupy or improve his allotment, the allotment could be leased for three-
year periods to outside parties certified by the government.
The second piece of legislation was the Miami Town Company Act of March 3, 1891, which authorized the secretary
of the interior to sell nearly 600 acres of strategically
located Ottawa land to the Miami Town Company for a
minimum of ten dollars per acre, with the proceeds to
go to the Ottawas on an individual basis. Like the Dawes
Act, both of these laws emphasized individual ownership
and responsibility. Under the general authority of the 1887
act they provided the immediate setting for the Ottawa
Allotment Act of 1892. By then most of the Ottawas had
taken white names, all spoke English, and only six of the

less than two hundred tribal members could be counted as full bloods. It was an indication of the subsequent acceleration of the assimilation process that only two of the original allottees held their land under federal trusteeship in 1927.[4]

During the tenure of Indian Commissioner Cato Sells from 1913 to 1921, the government aggressively pursued a program of declaring restricted Indians competent, especially in Oklahoma. The result was that 90 percent of the Ottawa allotments were sold, and population shifts to nearby towns and cities became commonplace. Nevertheless, some social and cultural cohesion was maintained by the retention of an eight-and-one-half-acre cemetery and the ceremonial election of a tribal chief. Since the Ottawas (like other Oklahoma and Alaska tribes) were excluded from those provisions of the Wheeler-Howard Act of 1934 that provided authority and funding for the reconstitution of defunct tribal organizations, they had to await passage of the Oklahoma Welfare Act of 1936 to revitalize their tribe as a recognized corporate body. This was formally accomplished in 1939. In the meantime, while membership in the Ottawa Baptist Church declined, the issue of the educational fraud in Kansas remained dormant, though it certainly was not forgotten. Eventually, the drive for legal atonement would become a rallying point for renewed interest in the Ottawa language and tribal traditions.[5]

Informed Ottawas remained adamant in their belief that they had been defrauded of money, educational opportunity, and valuable reservation land in Franklin County, Kansas. The problem was that in the absence of congressional authorization it was legally impossible to petition for redress in the United States Court of Claims. Their complaints were anything but popular, and as a small tribe with limited political influence in the conservative, Bible-belt setting of Kansas and Oklahoma, it was virtually impossible to obtain political support for the required enabling legislation. Their predicament, of course, was not unlike that of scores of similar Indian groups throughout the land—legally constituted Indian communities whose members had enjoyed full United States citizenship since 1924, had served in two World Wars, and had been led to believe that America was the very bastion of equality and justice. Above all else, they believed that the legal system of the United States could in fact accommodate moral questions whose basic precepts were simple and clear.

Because of strongly expressed sentiment of that sort, and the more practical effect of public pressure directed at the legal bottleneck created by the 1863 Court of Claims restriction regarding Indian claims, President Truman signed the Indian Claims Commission Act on August 13, 1946. Now Indian people could at least be given a hearing regarding claims of law or equity under the Constitution, laws, treaties, and executive orders. They could also be heard in law or equity claims under sounding of tort, fraudlent claims under treaty or other contractual arrangements, and claims based upon reasonable and honorable dealings not recognized by prevailing law or equity. In short, the law contemplated the application of legal and moral arguments in the determination of just compensation.[6]

A significant obstacle to the pursuit of any Ottawa claim was the question whether an Ottawa nation had existed prior to and following white contact. The resolution of that issue was difficult, because any specific petition was certain to prompt additional petitions and counterpetitions from the various organized Ottawa groups and would endanger what the Oklahoma Ottawas believed to be their exclusive, rightful claim to damages under the treaties of 1862 and 1867. For them it was essential to demonstrate that the Ottawas of Blanchard's Fork and Roche de Boeuf were in fact separate tribal entities, with exclusive rights that could not be claimed by the Ottawas of Michigan or elsewhere. In at least half a dozen treaties from 1795 to the mid-1830s it had been in the best interest of the United States vaguely to designate the various Ottawa groups as "the Ottawas," "the Ottawa tribe or nation," "the Ottawa nation," or "the United Nation of Chippewa, Ottawa and

Potawatomi Indians." On occasion, they were more specifically identified by geographic location or village organization, but that did little to clarify the issue of alleged
nationality and the government's legal obligations to specific families, clans, or groups.[7]

The extended legal history that eventually led to a settlement for the Oklahoma Ottawas began on August 22, 1949,
when Petitions 40-B, C, D, E, and F were filed with the
Indian Claims Commission by "Robert Dominic, et. al., as
the representatives and on behalf of all members by blood
of The Ottawa Tribe of Indians," asserting, either as the
purported successor to or on behalf of "The Ottawa Tribe,"
financial claims based on the treaties of August 3, 1795,
July 4, 1805, November 17, 1807, September 29, 1817,
and August 29, 1821. The essence of Dominic's plea, which
had the support of the "Northern Michigan Ottawa Organization," was that no tribal organization recognized by the
secretary of the interior existed with authority to represent
all of the descendants of the Ottawa nation, or tribe, of
Indians who resided in several states of the union, and that
specific claims under the named treaties could only be
sought by specific groups who could be identified by a clear
blood succession.

Less than two years later, on July 6, 1951, a petition
captioned "The Ottawa Tribe, and Guy Jennison, Bronson
Edwards and Gene Jennison, as representatives of The
Ottawa Tribe v. The United States of America" was filed
with the Claims Commission. Representing the position of
the Oklahoma Ottawas (Guy Jennison was allottee number
77 on the 1892 Allotment Roll and a ⅜-blood Ottawa),
the petition alleged that the Ottawa Tribe of Oklahoma
was a bona fide tribal organization recognized by the secretary of the interior as having full authority to represent
the tribe and all its members. The Jennisons and Edwards
appeared on the petition "only for the purpose of obtaining
a full judgment on all the issues, if it should be determined
that the [Oklahoma] Ottawa Tribe [was] not now organized
with capacity to sue in its own name." Excluding the 1795

claim, all treaties listed in the Dominic petition were now claimed as the exclusive litigious domain of the Oklahoma Ottawas, who further asserted that the Michigan and/or United Tribe Ottawas (and their descendants) were not members of The Ottawa Tribe. In short, in the words of the Claims Commission, "The essence of such pleadings . . . was the presentation of identical claims by two separate groups contending to have sole right to bring said actions for the Ottawa Tribe."[8]

Following a preliminary hearing on November 7, 1951, and subsequent hearings on March 11 and October 14, 1952, the Claims Commission issued its final opinion on August 6, 1953. As in the majority of cases before the Claims Commission, it was stated that determination of the issue necessitated recounting the history of the Ottawa Indians. Citing the research of ethnologist William Bernon Kinietz (which was based on evidence dating back to the early seventeenth century), the precise wordings of the various treaties in question, the several recorded statements of Chief Kewaygushcam of the Grand River (Michigan) Band, and annuity receipts maintained by the General Accounting Office, the Commission concluded,

> This entire record indicates that there was no chief of the entire nation, nor general council of the entire nation of Ottawas having control over any lands as belonging to the entire nation; but that different bands of Ottawas occupied and had the authority to dispose of different sections of land, though other bands of Ottawas may have had some interest therein. In fact, it would seem from the cessions themselves that the lands conveyed were frequently jointly owned, not only by different bands of Ottawas, but also by Chippewas, Pottawatomies, and sometimes by Wyandottes and other tribes. . . . The only treaty that seems, from the record, to have been recognized as belonging to one band of Ottawas alone is the treaty of August 29, 1821; and that it was recognized as belonging solely to the Grand River Band of Michigan is indicated by the fact that the annuity of $1,000 provided therein was

thereafter paid to this band alone, and the payment of said
annuity ceased after the release by this band in the treaty of
1855.[9]

In its "Finding of Facts," the Claims Commission also
demonstrated that before 1821 only the Blanchard's Fork
and Roche de Boeuf groups had been entitled to annuities
under the treaties of 1795, 1805, 1807, 1817, and 1818;
they had even received some annuities under the 1821
treaty, though the payments had been contrary to the
letter of the law. In any case, the commission concluded
that the Blanchard's Fork and Roche de Boeuf Ottawas
enjoyed a "larger interest" in all of the pre-1821 treaties,
and in effect, they were the closest of the different bands
to being a chronologically sustained Ottawa tribe that
could be identified under law. This did not mean, of
course, that they constituted the possibly mythical Ottawa
nation; they simply were more central to the long sweep
of Ottawa history than the other bands. The 1831, 1862,
and 1867 treaties were made a part of the official record
in the 1953 decision, and since in these treaties the
Blanchard's Fork and Roche de Boeuf bands were very
clearly and exclusively identified, the Oklahoma Ottawas
were in an enviable position to pursue their claims in
Kansas without fear of counterpetitions from other Ottawa groups.[10]

In fact, they had done that, well in advance of the
1953 ruling. On August 10, 1951, the Oklahoma group
had filed a petition with the Claims Commission, entitled "Trust Lands in Kansas," which was designated
separate ICC Docket No. 303. Carefully noting that none
of the 303 claims were then pending in any court of the
United States, the docket listed the individual petitioners—
Guy Jennison, Bronson Edwards, and Gene Jennison—as
representatives of the Ottawa Tribe, in a manner similar
to ICC Docket No. 133, which, of course, was then still
pending. The claims under 303 arose out of the 1862 and
1867 treaties, and in a section titled "The Ottawa Tribe"

the damaged groups were identified as those specific groups who in good faith had entered into the 1831 treaty, i.e., "the band of Ottaway Indians, residing on Blanchard's Fork of the Great Auglaize River, and at Oquanoxa's village, the band of Ottaway Indians, residing at or near the places called Roche de Boeuf and Wolf rapids, in the Miami river of Lake Erie, and within the State of Ohio." To strengthen their case, it was further stated that, after these bands had been "reunited" in the future Kansas Territory, they had on occasion been referred to as the "Ottawas of Kansas" and at other times as "the Ottawas of Blanchard's Fork and Roche de Boeuf." Pursuant to the 1862 and 1867 treaties, they were again removed under federal supervision and redesignated "The Ottawa Tribe of Oklahoma," which was given even firmer government sanction under authority of the Oklahoma Indian Welfare Act of 1936. In short, the plaintiff attorneys in Docket 303 left few stones unturned in attempting to establish the legal identity of their clients.[11]

The petition of August 10, 1951, was an informed and comprehensive summary of violations the Ottawas purportedly had suffered during their residence in Kansas. In the several causes of action the principal charges were that the government had:

(1) allowed the assets of Ottawa University to be dissipated through secretive and fraudulent sales of university land;

(2) allowed sales to be completed without maintaining proper accounting procedures;

(3) allowed funds received from the sale of university land and money donated by white citizens for Ottawa welfare to be dissipated;

(4) permitted land patents to be issued for lands sold under fraudulent conditions;

(5) permitted the organization of an illegal university board of trustees and sanctioned the operation of this illegal board;

(6) failed to guarantee that Ottawa University would always be open to Ottawa children;

(7) never provided the Ottawa Tribe with a full accounting of the final disposition of all trust lands sold under the 1862 and 1867 treaties;

(8) allowed the purported "settlement" of October 29, 1873, which provided for only a small fraction of the university lands or trust lands remaining unsold to return to the tribe, and only a fraction of the assets obtained out of the proceeds of the land to return to the tribe;

(9) allowed the tribe to pay for several investigations of the aforesaid violations, and allowed the secretary of the interior to control their attorneys;

(10) permitted the Ottawa Tribe to be deprived of more than 20,000 acres of its best land and of the value and benefits thereof;

(11) failed to protect the tribe from taxation by the state of Kansas; and

(12) continuously dealt with the Ottawa Tribe in an unfair and dishonorable manner, to the petitioners' damage.

Other related complaints were listed. Particularly significant was the thirty-sixth and final cause, which charged that under the treaties of 1862 and 1867 the Ottawa Tribe had been subjected to "duress" and repeatedly had been misinformed and mistaken as to the actual facts and nature of those treaties. Falling under the rubric of the Claims Commission Act that allowed consideration for "unconscionable" treatment, this complaint would eventually prove critical in the final determination of Docket 303.[12]

The task of collecting the necessary evidence in support of these complaints was enormous. Records were scattered from Kansas to Washington and often were filed in the confusing bureaucratic style that researchers have come to accept as typical of Indian record keeping in the nineteenth century. Thus it was hardly to be expected that a decision could be rendered in a few months, or even years. In addition, the early 1950s were characterized by increasing lethargy and procrastination in the completion of many ICC dockets. Attempts to clear those dockets were almost routinely stymied by a movement dating back to the 1940s calling for the dismantling of the Indian Bureau, the termination of all federal relations with Indian peoples, and in the broadest and most simplistic sense, getting the government out of "the Indian business." During the administration of Indian Commissioner Dillon S. Myer (1950 to 1953)—whom former Interior Secretary Harold L. Ickes characterized as "Hitler and Mussolini rolled into one"—these new policies came to dominate Indian affairs. Aided and encouraged by Utah Senator Arthur Watkins and other conservative congressmen from the states with large Indian populations, Myer played a key role in the adoption of House Concurrent Resolution No. 108 of August 1, 1953, which named specific tribes which were to be terminated "at the earliest possible date." Additional guidelines were included for more long-range termination projects. Purportedly on grounds of economy, Commissioner Myer was also critical of ICC attorneys who had been or were being selected from areas other than the actual population centers of the various tribes. For example, the Oklahoma Ottawas had engaged the services of Harrison, Thomas, Spangenberg & Hull of Cleveland, Ohio. Although Myer denied before a Senate subcommittee that he had attempted to discourage the filing of claims before the announced August 13, 1951, expiration date of the Indian Claims Commission's authority, a recent study suggests that the charge was not groundless. Collectively, these circumstances further militated against any quick settlement of Docket 303.[13]

While the Ottawas were not one of the several tribes specifically designated for termination under HCR 108, congressional hearings the following year provided the political framework for extending the new policy to them. Unlike the Florida Seminoles, two-thirds of whose members were unable to speak English, the Ottawas were largely integrated into the dominant white culture and generally indistinguishable from their white neighbors in northeastern Oklahoma. There were no full-bloods in the tribe, and the majority could not claim the minimum quarter blood quantum required for government assistance programs. Only 558.64 acres of Ottawa land were still held in trust as individual allotments, and all but one of the eleven parcels involved were encumbered in various forms of heirship status. Yet there was concern over precisely what termination might mean for the tribe as a whole, particularly with regard to maintaining the tribal cemetery in Ottawa County, Oklahoma; hospital care; and educational benefits. Certainly, there was great concern over the possible outcome of ICC Docket No. 303.[14]

At this point in the legal proceedings the Ottawas were subjected to the kind of political intimidation and economic pressure reminiscent of their experiences in Kansas. Like the Wisconsin Menominees, many of whom supported termination in 1954 only after Senator Watkins and the Senate Subcommittee on Indian Affairs promised a $1,500 per capita payment from a recent Court of Claims settlement, some Ottawas agreed to termination only after they had been promised a speedy and favorable settlement of their claims before the ICC. This, of course, was clearly in violation of the legal authority of federal commissioners, senators, or anyone else—as were promises that after termination individual Ottawas would be eligible for Indian health and educational benefits whether or not they had the required blood quantum. One recent study of contemporary Ottawa affairs concludes that government representatives lied outright, but it is also possible that there was some misunderstanding or unintentional misrepresentation of federal regulations. In any case, the majority of the tribe supported termination and believed that such action would hasten the settlement of their claims with the government. Public Law 943, "An Act to Provide for the termination of Federal supervision over the property of the Ottawa Tribe of Indians in the State of Oklahoma and the individual members thereof, and for other purposes," went into effect on August 3, 1956, and provided that the 1938 charter to the Ottawa Tribe of Oklahoma would be revoked within three years. The tribe was instructed to prepare a final termination roll to be published in the *Federal Register* as the final enumeration of the Oklahoma Ottawa Tribe. As completed and submitted to the government on July 28, 1959, the roll listed 630 individuals, a substantial increment from the 488 count listed in the House report in 1953. Included were blood-quantum percentages ranging from 1/256 (three individuals) to ¾ (two individuals), with the majority falling above the ¼ quantum range. Obviously there was great interest in being included in this final count, especially since Section 10 of Public Law 943 stated that " [n]othing in this Act shall affect any claims heretofore filed against the United States."[15]

Legal atonement for the Ottawas moved a step closer with the filing of the plaintiffs' proposed findings of fact on July 1, 1957. In one of the most thorough records of fact ever filed with the Claims Commission, attorney Allan Hull submitted sixty-four pages of evidence describing how the Ottawas had been dispossessed of land, money, and especially educational facilities in Kansas. Citing the actions of Jones, Hutchinson, Kalloch, Atkinson, the University Board of Trustees, the Baptist Home Missionary Society, a variety of government officials, and several investigative bodies, Hull presented a comprehensive picture of how the government had violated its trust and how questionable legal maneuvers over an extended period of time had been used to defraud the Ottawas. Particularly damaging was Hull's recitation of a message from Interior Secretary Delano to Congress in December, 1872, in which the secretary had sought to justify his failure to take possession of the university and school property under the 1872 statute on grounds that too much pressure was being exerted by "some members of the Baptist Church." Complaining further of the erection of "a costly and unnecessary stone building in plain and palpable violation of the provisions of the trust as created by the [1862] treaty," Delano had in his own words concluded:

> The said trust . . . contemplated the education of the Ottawa Indians and their prosperity, while it is manifest that affairs

have been conducted with a view to the education of white persons principally, and that little or no benefit in the way of education has been obtained on behalf of the Indians. . . . The whole management of the trust-fund has been irregular and careless, if not *improvident* [emphasis added] and wasteful.[16]

It is doubtful that Hull and his associates caught the irony of Delano's reference to "improvident" management. Certainly they were not speaking of providence conceived by Isaac McCoy and Jotham Meeker a century earlier. After all, the Ottawa attorneys were more concerned with demonstrable fraud and the misuse of tribal funds than with the alleged workings of divine guidance among a people once considered uncivilized. But that is not to say that the moral dimension was ignored. In fact, a very basic legal strategy in Docket 303 was the application of the "fair and honorable dealings" section of the Indian Claims Commission Act, the provision that turned more on moral than legal questions. Having demonstrated that the government through its "responsible officials" had failed to take proper action when it was apparent that various trusts were being violated, attorney Hull argued that at the time of the Treaty of 1862 the Ottawas were not far enough advanced in education and the civilized arts to be able to understand how they were being systematically defrauded. Very few could read or understand English, and even fewer could understand the intricate transactions that denied them educational benefits while diminishing both the quantity and the value of their Kansas lands.[17]

When the long-awaited opinion of the Claims Commission was released on June 29, 1960, it upheld the plaintiffs' petition almost to the letter. As a matter of law, the Ottawas were entitled to recover:

- $30,603.94 for trust land funds unaccounted for by Agent Hutchinson, together with interest at between 4 and 5 percent;
- $22,600.00 for the Ottawa University section of land, and

- $7,490.00 for 1,280 acres illegally conveyed to Ottawa University;
- $3,354.75 in treaty funds not conveyed to the tribe by Agent Hutchinson;
- $1,202.42 for expenses the Ottawas had paid to the 1872 and 1873 commissions.

In addition, the Ottawas were awarded the actual appraised value of 10,702 acres of school lands (less whatever sums had been previously paid to the tribe), plus an amount equal to Hutchinson's and Kalloch's profits from the sale of 5,000 acres of Ottawa school land and the value of 3,032 acres of school lands sold by the university trustees, who had not invested the proceeds as required by the 1862 treaty. The keystone section sustaining the research and legal analysis of the Ottawa attorneys stated:

> There is no evidence that the officials of the Government ever first investigated to determine the capacity of the Ottawa Indians or the white trustees to manage and control an educational trust. Neither is there any evidence that there was any effort made to determine whether the Ottawa Indians were ready to take on the responsibilities of citizenship which the [1862] treaty provided they would obtain five years after ratification of the treaty. It is a fact, however, that at the time of the 1862 treaty their chiefs knew no English and only a few could speak the language. Under the circumstances there was a moral obligation on the part of the defendant to thoroughly check on their ability to face the responsibilities of citizenship and to administer a trust.[18]

While the opinion seemed clear and equitable, the possibility of an award of nearly $500,000 prompted defense attorneys to file a motion for a rehearing on October 14, 1960. The motion was denied the following March 10. Responding to the government's new argument that the case had been erroneously decided on moral grounds when it should have been determined primarily on legal grounds (which in themselves were questionable), the Claims Commission ruled that nothing in the findings militated against applying moral considerations as defined in Clause (5) Section 2 of the Indian Claims Commission Act: "We did not hold there was a fiduciary duty on the part of the United States based on legal principles," concluded the commission, "but rather one based on moral obligation." The commission was no less blunt in denying the defendant's additional claim that "The Ottawa Indians were probably further advanced in civilization at the date of the execution of the 1862 treaty than any of the Indian tribes that were located in the Kansas Territory [sic]" and thus able to manage and control a trust. In support of that claim, the government had submitted newspaper clippings detailing the growth of the town of Ottawa, the sale of Ottawa lands, delinquent tax lists, and stories regarding the history of Ottawa University as "new evidence." The eighty-seven such exhibits submitted were cumulative, said the commission, and could not meet the requirements of Section 33 (b) 3 of the ICC's General Rules of Procedure.[19]

The defendant's appeal to the United States Court of Claims was certiorari denied by the United States Supreme Court on December 7, 1964. After additional findings dealing with legal offsets in the amount of $2,028.77 and the interest to be computed on the $30,603.94 of unaccounted-for Hutchinson trust funds, the commission ordered its amended final award on February 11, 1965. The award came to a total of $406,166.19 and was appropriated by Congress on the following April 30. The final disposition of these nontaxable funds on a per-capita basis to the 630 members of the Ottawa Tribe of Oklahoma was governed by Public Law 90-63, approved by Congress on August 11, 1967. Legal atonement, if not absolute restitution, had finally been achieved.[20]

Today the Baptist denomination continues to operate Ottawa University in Franklin County, Kansas. White farmers cultivate the fertile hinterland that once was the Ottawa Indian reservation. Tauy Jones Hall still graces the well-manicured university campus and stands as a symbol to local Baptists of a noble and worthy past. Clinton C. Hutchinson, Isaac Kalloch, Robert Atkinson, and Enoch Hoag are largely forgotten, as are the legal wars of the past. The university's Department of Religion offers a full complement of courses designed to acquaint students with ethics, Christianity, and morality. A few Ottawas have enrolled under the University's Indian scholarship program, but for the most part the tribe looks elsewhere for the education of their youth. That seems an understandable response to events of the past.[21]

Notes

Chapter 1. Searching for Lost Justice

1. George Washington, "Farewell Address," September 17, 1796, in James D. Richardson, comp., *A Compilation of the Messages and Papers of the Presidents* 1:212.

2. Cited in Gail Kennedy, ed., *Education for Democracy: The Debate over the Report of the President's Commission on Higher Education*, p. 3.

3. Daniel J. Boorstin, *The Americans: The National Experience*, p. 155.

4. Cited in ibid., p. 154.

5. Theron Baldwin in *Thirteenth Annual Report of the Society for the Promotion of Collegiate and Theological Education in the West* (1856), cited in Donald G. Tewksbury, *The Funding of American Colleges and Universities before the Civil War*, p. 5.

6. Boorstin, *The Americans*, p. 156; Tewksbury, *Founding of American Colleges and Universities*, table 2, p. 28.

7. The results of the most recent and thorough investigation of the Ottawa fraud are in *The Ottawa Tribe and Guy Jennison, Bronson Edwards and Gene Jennison, as Representatives of the Ottawa Tribe* vs. *The United States of America*, Doc. No. 303, in Indian Claims Commission, *Indian Claims Commission Decisions* 14:677-78.

8. See, for example, Grant Foreman, *The Last Trek of the Indians*, and H. Craig Miner and William E. Unrau, *The End of Indian Kansas: A Study of Cultural Revolution, 1854-1871*.

9. For example, Wilcomb E. Washburn, *Red Man's Land/White Man's Law*; Wilbur R. Jacobs, *Dispossessing the American Indian: Indians and Whites on the Colonial Frontier*; and Paul Wallace Gates, *Fifty Million Acres: Conflicts over Kansas Land Policy, 1854-1890*.

10. Special Subcommittee on Indian Education, Committee on Labor and Public Welfare, *Indian Education: A National Tragedy —A National Challenge*, 91st Cong., 1st Sess., 1969, Senate Report no. 501.

11. "Clarification of Ottawa Indian Financial Aid Procedures," memo from W. L. Pankratz to [Ottawa University] Administrative Council, April 18, 1977, Office of Financial Aid, Ottawa University, Ottawa, Kansas, in Russ Driver, ed., *1976-1977 Catalog Issue of the Ottawa University Bulletin* 73, no. 1.

12. Charles J. Kappler, comp., *Indian Affairs, Laws and Treaties* 2:831.

13. *The Oxford English Dictionary* 4:516.

14. Francis Jennings, *The Invasion of America: Indians, Colonialism, and the Cant of Conquest*, p. vii.

Chapter 2. The Ottawas and the Invader

1. Kappler, *Indian Affairs*, 2:830-34; Charles C. Royce, comp., *Indian Land Cessions in the United States*, pt. 2, plate 157.

2. "Defendant's Request for Findings of Fact," Doc. 133, Indian Claims Commission, *The Ottawa Tribe and Guy Jennison, et. al. v. United States*, copy, Library Division, Kansas State Historical Society, Topeka.

3. Docs. 13-F, 15-I, 18-K, 27, 29, 64-A, 89, 133, 141, 308, and 341-D and 30 Ind. Cl. Cm. 337, *Indian Claims Commission Decisions*, 30:337-71.

4. Johanna E. Feest and Christian F. Feest, "Ottawa," in Bruce G. Trigger, ed., *Northeast*, vol. 15 of William C. Sturtevant, ed., *Handbook of North American Indians*, p. 785.

5. Joseph H. Cash and Gerald W. Wolff, *The Ottawa People*, p. 99.

6. Edward G. Bourne, ed., and Annie N. Bourne, trans., *The Voyages and Explorations of Samuel de Champlain, 1604-1616* 1:66, 100-101.

7. Reuben Gold Thwaites, ed., *The Jesuit Relations and Allied Documents, Travels and Explorations of the Jesuit Missionaries in*

New France, 39:15, 49:241, 54:169, 55:133.

8. Henry R. Schoolcraft, *Historical Sketches and Statistical Information Respecting the History, Condition and Prospects of the Indian Tribes of the United States*, pt. 1, p. 478; Feest and Feest, "Ottawa," p. 772; Cash and Wolff, *Ottawa People*, p. 1. A seventeenth-century English source defines trade as "[A]n Art of Getting, Preparing, and Exchanging things Commodious for Humane Necessities and Convenience." See *The Oxford English Dictionary*, 11: 224.

9. R. David Edmunds, *The Potawatomis: Keepers of the Fire*, p. 3; Feest and Feest, "Ottawa," p. 772; Louise Barry, comp., *The Beginning of the West: Annals of the Kansas Gateway to the American West, 1540-1854* pp. 313, 550, 943; Johnston Lykins to Jotham Meeker, July 27, 1842, and Meeker to S. Peck, May 6, 1845, December 31, 1846, January 25, 1848, Jotham Meeker Papers, Manuscript Division, Kansas State Historical Society, Topeka (microfilm, R 1 and 2); Doc. 303, Indian Claims Commission, *The Ottawa Tribe and Guy Jennison, et. al. v. United States*, p. 41, copy, Library Division, Kansas State Historical Society. Jones apparently had some competency in all three dialects, though he appears to have been weaker in Potawatomi. Writing to the Ottawa Baptist missionary in Kansas in 1842, the Reverend Johnston Lykins refused to certify Jones as a translator for the "Bible Society," pointing out that "Jones continually falls into this error [of pronouncing Potawatomi incorrectly], insisting always that he gave pure Putawatomi [*sic*]." Lykins further stated that Jones's knowledge of Ottawa and Chippewa served as an impediment to his correct use of Potawatomi. See Lykins to Meeker, July 27, 1842, Meeker Papers (R 1, F 0760-1).

10. Edmunds, *The Potawatomis*, pp. 3-4.

11. Feest and Feest, "Ottawa," p. 772; Schoolcraft, *Historical and Statistical Information*, p. 478; Lewis Henry Morgan, *The Indian Journals, 1859-62*, ed. Leslie A. White, p. 39; *Robert Dominic, et. al., as the representatives and on behalf of all members by blood of The Ottawa Tribe of Indians v. United States of America, Indian Claims Commission Decisions*, 2:469, 473-74; Cash and Wolff, *Ottawa People*, pp. 10-11.

12. Feest and Feest, "Ottawa," p. 774; Cash and Wolff, *Ottawa People*, p. 8.

13. Cash and Wolff, *Ottawa People*, pp. 8-9; Paul Chrisler Phillips, *The Fur Trade*, 1:457-58.

14. Phillips, *The Fur Trade*, 1:456.

15. E. Wagner Stearn and Allen E. Stearn, *The Effect of Small-pox on the Destiny of the Amerindian*, pp. 21, 29, 51, and 65. For a study of the advent of epidemic disease among the Algonquians, see Sherburne F. Cook, "The Significance of Disease in the Extinction of the New England Indians," *Human Biology*, 45 (1973): 485-508.

16. James A. Clifton, *The Prairie People: Continuity and Change in Potawatomi Indian Culture, 1665-1965*, pp. 70-72; Edmunds, *The Potawatomis*, pp. 36-37.

17. Clifton, *The Prairie People*, pp. 93-97; Feest and Feest, "Ottawa," pp. 773-74; Edmunds, *The Potawatomis*, pp. 41-42.

18. Howard H. Peckham, *Pontiac and the Indian Uprising*, pp. 40-56; Jacobs, *Dispossessing the American Indian*, pp. 75-93; Feest and Feest, "Ottawa," p. 774.

19. Randolph C. Downes, *Council Fires on the Upper Ohio*, pp. 240-41; Edmunds, *The Potawatomis*, pp. 111-12.

20. Entry for October 15, 1785, *Journals of the Continental Congress, 1774-1789*, ed. Gailland Hunt, 25:680-93; Edmunds, *The Potawatomis*, pp. 116-34; Reginald Horsman, *Expansion and American Indian Policy, 1783-1812*, p. 98.

21. Kappler, *Indian Affairs*, 2:39-45; Horsman, *Expansion and American Indian Policy*, pp. 101-103; Cash and Wolff, *Ottawa People*, p. 9.

22. Kappler, *Indian Affairs*, 2:92-95, 99-100, 117-19, 145-55, 162-63, 198-201, 335-39.

23. Malcolm J. Rohrbough, *The Land Office Business: The Settlement and Administration of American Public Lands, 1789-1837*, pp. 17, 23; Clifton, *The Prairie People*, 179.

24. Kappler, *Indian Affairs*, 2:92-95, 99-100; Jefferson to Senate of the United States, January 15, 1808, *American State Papers, Class II: Indian Affairs*, 2:746-47; Horsman, *Expansion and American Indian Policy*, p. 155.

25. Edmunds, *The Potawatomis*, 165-77; Horsman, *Expansion and American Indian Policy*, pp. 165-69.

26. Henry R. Schoolcraft, *Personal Memoirs of a Residence of Thirty Years With the Indian Tribes on the American Frontiers: With Brief Notices of Passing Events, Facts, and Opinions. A.D. 1812 to A.D. 1842*, p. 483.

27. Kappler, *Indian Affairs*, 2:117-19; Edmunds, *The Potawatomis*, p. 205.

28. Graham to Cass, March 23, 1817, Kappler, *Indian Affairs*, 2: 136.

29. Kappler, *Indian Affairs*, 2:145-55, 162-63; Cass and McArthur to Graham, September 30, 1817, Graham to Cass and McArthur, October 17, 1817, in Kappler, *Indian Affairs*, 2:139-40; Paul W. Gates, "Indian Allotments Preceding the Dawes Act," in John G. Clark, ed., *The Frontier Challenge: Responses to the Trans-Mississippi West*, pp. 147-48.

30. Kappler, *Indian Affairs*, 2:150.

31. Francis P. Prucha, *American Indian Policy in the Formative Years: The Indian Trade and Intercourse Acts, 1790-1834*, p. 220; Bernard W. Sheehan, *Seeds of Extinction: Jeffersonian Philanthropy and the American Indians*, p. 274; "Trade, Intercourse, and Schools," a communication to the House of Representatives, January 22, 1818, in Kappler, *Indian Affairs*, 2:150-51.

32. *U.S. Stat.*, 3:515-17; Prucha, *American Indian Policy*, p. 222.

33. Kappler, *Indian Affairs*, 2:198-201; Edmunds, *The Potawatomis*, pp. 220-21; Herman Viola, *Thomas L. McKenney, Architect of America's Early Indian Policy, 1816-1830*, p. 197; George A. Schultz, *An Indian Canaan: Isaac McCoy and the Vision of an Indian State*, p. 54.

Chapter 3. Providence and Removal

1. L. Bolles to Isaac McCoy, February 19, 1833, Isaac McCoy Papers, Manuscript Division, Kansas State Historical Society, Topeka (microfilm edition, R 8).

2. Sheehan, *Seeds of Extinction*, pp. 246, 276-77; Andrew Jackson, message to Congress, December 8, 1829, in Richardson, comp., *Messages and Papers*, 3:1021.

3. Jedidiah Morse, *Report to the Secretary of War of the United States, on Indian Affairs*, pp. 11-13, 19-21, 76-79, 83, 284-90.

4. "Progress Made in Civilizing the Indians," John C. Calhoun to Hon. H. Clay, communicated to the House of Representatives, January 17, 1820, in Kappler, *Indian Affairs*, 2:200-201. For opposition to the "Civilization Fund," see Prucha, *American Indian Policy*, pp. 222-23.

5. "Application of the Board of Commissioners for Foreign Missions for Pecuniary Aid in Civilizing Indians," communicated to the House of Representatives, March 3, 1824, in Kappler, *Indian Affairs*, 2:446. See also Robert F. Berkhofer, Jr., *Salvation and the Savage: An Analysis of Protestant Missions and American Indian Response, 1787-1862*.

182 NOTES TO PAGES 39-47

6. Minutes of the Baptist Board, April 26, 1822, cited in Berk-hofer, *Salvation and the Savage*, pp. 7-8.

7. Smith, Platt, Morse, Van Rensselaer, and Evarts to Senate and House of Representatives, March 3, 1824, in Kappler, *Indian Affairs*, 2:447.

8. "Civilization of Indians," communication to the House of Representatives, March 23, 1824, in Kappler, *Indian Affairs*, 2:457-59.

9. "Proposition to Extinguish Indian Title to Lands in Missouri," communicated to the Senate, May 14, 1824, Kappler, *Indian Affairs*, 2:512; Prucha, *American Indian Policy*, pp. 224-25.

10. "Proposition to Extinguish Indian Title," in Kappler, *Indian Affairs*, 2:512.

11. Kappler, *Indian Affairs*, 2:217-25.

12. Calhoun to President of the United States, January 24, 1825, and President James Monroe to the Senate, January 27, 1825, in Kappler, *Indian Affairs*, 2:541-44; Prucha, *American Indian Policy*, pp. 224-27; Prucha, "Thomas McKenney and the New York Indian Board," *Mississippi Valley Historical Review* 48 (March, 1962): 635-55; Viola, *Thomas L. McKenney*, pp. 200-19; Schultz, *An Indian Canaan*, p. 99.

13. Thwaites, *Jesuit Relations*, 1:32-33, 39:15, 49:241-45, 50: 285-91, 54:169-75, 55:133.

14. George Paré, "The St. Joseph Mission," *Mississippi Valley Historical Review* 17 (June, 1930): 24-54.

15. Schultz, *An Indian Canaan*, pp. 3-58; "statements of the expenditures made under the act to provide for the civilization of the Indian tribes," 1820 and 1823, and "statement in relation to establishments in the Indian country for the purpose of civilizing the Indians," 1824, in Kappler, *Indian Affairs*, 2:272, 443, 459; "Introduction to the Isaac McCoy Papers," R 1, microfilm edition, ed. Joseph W. Snell (Topeka: Kansas State Historical Society, 1967).

16. Schultz, *An Indian Canaan*, pp. 64-65; "statement showing the number of Indian schools, where established, by whom, the number of teachers . . . and the amount paid to each by the Government," December 3, 1825, in Kappler, *Indian Affairs*, 2:587.

17. Isaac McCoy, *History of Baptist Missions: Embracing Remarks on the Former and Present Condition of the Aboriginal Tribes: Their Former Settlement Within the Indian Territory, and Their Future Prospects*, p. 133.

18. John W. McGee, *The Catholic Church in the Grand River Valley, 1833-1950*, pp. 37-38; Robert Bolt, "Reverend Leonard Slater in the Grand Valley," *Michigan History* 51 (Fall, 1967):

241–48.

19. Simerwell to McCoy, April 12, 1832, McCoy Papers (microfilm ed., R 1).

20. McKenney to Barbour, December 27, 1826, in Kappler, *Indian Affairs*, 2:700.

21. Viola, *Thomas L. McKenney*, pp. 211–14; Schultz, *An Indian Canaan*, pp. 99–104.

22. "Thoughts Respecting the Indian Territory," Saint Louis, August 6, 1828, McCoy Papers (R 6); Schultz, *An Indian Canaan*, p. 104.

23. McCoy to William Clark, October 7, 1828, and McCoy to McKenney, October 18, 1828, McCoy Papers (R 6).

24. McCoy to McLean, February 16, 1829, McCoy to Cass, September 11, 1829, and McCoy to Honorable Senate and House of Representatives of the United States, December 5, 1829, all in McCoy Papers (R 7).

25. Kappler, *Indian Affairs*, 2:294–97. An indication of the desperate situation at Carey was the official accounting for the year 1826, which indicated that $8,568.17 had been expended and only $4,948.68 received from all sources. "Abstract of Expenditures and Receipts by the Treasure of the General Convention of the Baptist Denomination for Foreign Missions, Etc., from April 1826 to April 1829, McCoy Papers (R 7).

26. Gosa, Shkaw-boos, Shmg-ur-rik, Sob-e-quam, Pe-wosh, and Kosh-quon-tkey (their marks) to President of the United States, February 17, 1829, McCoy Papers (R 7).

27. Prucha, *American Indian Policy*, pp. 233–44; Schultz, *An Indian Canaan*, pp. 129–34; McCoy to son, May 27, 1830, McCoy Papers (R 7).

28. *Correspondence on the Subject of the Emigration of Indians, between the 30th November, 1831, and 27 December, 1833, with Abstracts of Expenditures by Disbursing Agents in the Removal and Subsistence of Indians, etc., etc.*, 2:87–88.

29. Kappler, *Indian Affairs*, 2:310–18, 325–39.

30. Ibid., pp. 335–39.

31. McCoy to Lucius Bolles, December 1, 1830, McCoy to Eaton, March 2, 1831, McCoy to Bolles, March 25, 1833, McCoy to Spencer H. Cone, October 20, 1833, all in McCoy Papers (R 7 and 8); Schultz, *An Indian Canaan*, pp. 157, 172–73; Prucha, *American Indian Policy*, p. 272.

32. Barry, *Beginning of the West*, pp. 217, 223–34; Joseph B. King, "The Ottawa Indians in Kansas and Oklahoma," *Collections*

of the *Kansas State Historical Society* 13 (1913-14): 373-75; Edward E. Hill, *The Office of Indian Affairs, 1824-1880: Historical Sketches*, 64-66. See also the following articles by Robert F. Bauman: "The Migration of the Ottawa Indians from the Maumee Valley to Walpole Island," *Northwest Ohio Quarterly* 21 (Spring, 1949):86-112; "Kansas, Canada, or Starvation," *Michigan History* 36 (September, 1952): 287-99; "The Removal of the Indians from the Maumee Valley: A Selection from the Dresden W. H. Howard Papers," *Northwest Ohio Quarterly* 30 (Winter, 1957-58): 10-25.

33. Barry, *Beginning of the West*, pp. 250-51, 274, 334; "Unratified Treaty of November 12, 1833 (Fort Leavenworth)," RG 75, T 494, R 8, Documents Relating to the Negotiations of Ratified and Unratified Treaties with Various Tribes of Indians, Unratified Treaties, 1821-1865, National Archives.

34. Kappler, *Indian Affairs*, 2:392-94.

35. Schultz, *An Indian Canaan*, pp. 168-69, 172-73, 186-88; statements of McCoy, February 1 and 28, 1837, McCoy Papers (R 9).

36. Bauman, "Kansas, Canada, or Starvation," pp. 293-94; Bauman, "Removal of the Indians from the Maumee Valley," p. 13; Barry, *Beginning of the West*, p. 389; Schultz, *An Indian Canaan*, pp. 190-91, 197, 201.

Chapter 4. Wilderness Entrepreneurs

1. Schultz, *An Indian Canaan*, pp. 198-99.

2. *Baptist Banner and Western Pioneer—Extra* (Lexington, Kentucky), June 18, 1842, clipping, Jotham Meeker Papers, Manuscript Division, Kansas State Historical Society (microfilm ed., R. 1); Schultz, *An Indian Canaan*, p. 201.

3. Meeker to S. W. Lynd and G. H. Miller, September 22, 1842, Meeker Papers (R 1).

4. Johnston Lykins to Meeker, March 22, 1842; Notino, Komechaw, Petonuknout, Waweeshgua, and Ahshowissa to T. Hartley Crawford, December 1, 1843; Simpson and Hunter (Westport) to Meeker, December 25, 1845, all in Meeker Papers (R 1); Douglas C. McMurtrie and Albert H. Allen, *Jotham Meeker, Pioneer Printer of Kansas*, p. 18; Schultz, *An Indian Canaan*, pp. 91, 135; McCoy to L. Bolles, March 25, 1833, McCoy Papers (R 1).

5. "Introduction to the Meeker Papers," microfilm ed., R 1; McMurtrie and Allen, *Jotham Meeker*, pp. 16-36; Schultz, *An In-*

NOTES TO PAGES 62-67   185

dian Canaan, pp. 119, 154; McCoy to L. Bolles, March 25, 1833,
McCoy Papers (R 8); B. Smith Haworth, *Ottawa University: Its
History and Its Spirit,* pp. 1-4.
   6. Meeker to L. Bolles, February 27, 1841, Meeker Papers
(R 1); Schultz, *An Indian Canaan,* p. 198.
   7. Barry, *Beginning of the West,* p. 327; Ronald N. Satz, "Carey
Allen Harris," in Robert M. Kvasnicka and Herman J. Viola, eds.,
The Commissioners of Indian Affairs, 1824-1977, p. 20; Meeker
to L. Bolles, November 22, 1840, Meeker Papers (R 1).
   8. *Baptist Missionary Magazine* 18, no. 6 (June, 1838): 140, and
20, no. 11 (November, 1840): 262-63; Meeker to L. Bolles, July
8, 1840, Meeker Papers (R 1).
   9. Barry, *Beginning of the West,* pp. 327, 549-50; Robert E.
Starburg, "Baptists on the Kansas Frontier," B.D. thesis, Northern
Baptist Theological Seminary, 1960, typescript in Library Division,
Kansas State Historical Society, pp. 85-89, 122; *Baptist Missionary
Magazine* 27, no. 7 (July, 1847): 260.
   10. Meeker to S. Peck, February 1, 1848; Komchaw, Pahtu, and
Ahshowissa to Thomas H. Harvey, February 8, 1848; Peck to Meeker, March 22, 1848, all in Meeker Papers (R 2).
   11. *Baptist Missionary Magazine* 29, no. 7 (July, 1849): 270;
30, no. 11 (November, 1848): 403-404; and 32, no. 7 (July, 1852):
296.
   12. Schoolcraft, *Historical Sketches,* pp. 478-83; Schultz, *An Indian Canaan,* p. 198.
   13. John G. Pratt to Meeker, June 7 and July 7, 1853, Meeker
to George Manypenny, 1853, Meeker to George Manypenny, January 16, 1864, Meeker to Burton A. James, September 4, 1854,
Eleanor D. Meeker to Sister, 1855, all in Meeker Papers (R 2);
Schultz, *An Indian Canaan,* p. 198; Barry, *Beginning of the West,*
p. 1212; Haworth, *Ottawa University,* p. 4. Meeker was not alone
among missionaries responding to the economic pressure of their
positions. Christian Metz, representing the German Inspirations,
came to Kansas in 1854 and tried to buy lands from the Delawares
for a colony. After the Kansas colony failed, Metz's group established the Amana colonies in Iowa. Father Peter Henry Lemke,
founder of the Benedictine Order in Kansas, had to be constantly
reminded by superiors not to allow lot speculation to interfere with
his relationship to God. Metz's diary is in the Amana Historical
Society, Middle Amana, Iowa. Information on Lemke can be found
in Peter Beckman, *Kansas Monks: A History of St. Benedict's Abbey,*
pp. 13-17, 21. For an analysis of Commissioner Manypenny's role

in the land-cession treaties of the mid-1850s, see Miner and Unrau, *The End of Indian Kansas*, pp. 8–16.

14. Sheehan, *Seeds of Extinction*, p. 148.

15. Meeker to S. Peck, April 30, 1847, Meeker Papers (R 2).

16. John T. Jones to Secretary of the Interior, December 12, 1870, RG 75, M 234, R 658, Ottawa Agency, National Archives; Meeker to S. Peck, May 6, 1845, December 9, 1847, January 15, 1848, Meeker Papers (R 1 and 2); Robert Simerwell to Isaac Mc-Coy, April 12, 1832, McCoy Papers (R 7); A. T. Andreas, *The History of the State of Kansas*, pp. 304–305; Haworth, *Ottawa University*, pp. 4–6; Mrs. Shelly D. Rouse, "Colonel Dick Johnson's Choctaw Academy: A Forgotten Education Experiment," *Ohio Archeological and Historical Society Publication* 35 (January, 1916): 89.

17. Johnston Lykins to Meeker, July 27, 1842, and Meeker to Peck, December 31, 1846, December 9, 1847, January 15, 1848, Meeker Papers (R 1 and 2); Burton A. James to George Manypenny, March 10, 1854, RG 75, M 234, R 733, Sac and Fox Agency, National Archives; Barry, *Beginning of the West*, p. 550.

18. Meeker to Peck, December 13, 1846, January 15 and October 3, 1848, and Peck to Meeker, March 22, 1848, Meeker Papers (R 2); Barry, *Beginning of the West*, p. 735.

19. Meeker to Peck, January 15 and February 1, 1848; Komchan (Kom-o-chaw or Kom-Chaw), Pahtu (Pahtee), and Ahshowissa (Ottawa chiefs) to William Harvey, February 8, 1848; Mrs. John T. Jones to Meeker, May 29, 1848, all in Meeker Papers (R 2).

20. Meeker to Peck, February 28, 1848, Meeker Papers (R 2); John R. Chenault to Luke Lea, August 25, 1851, RG 75, M 234, R 733, Sac and Fox Agency, National Archives.

21. John G. Pratt to Meeker, July 7, 1853, Meeker to Peck, December 23, 1853, Meeker Papers (R 2); Perry Fuller to A. B. Greenwood, July 4, 1859, RG 75, M 234, R 734, Sac and Fox Agency, National Archives.

22. Ottawa Council to Manypenny, November 9, 1854, B. A. James to Manypenny, August 9, 1855, Ottawa Council (certified by Reverend John G. Pratt) to Commissioner of Indian Affairs, April 24, 1855, RG 75, M 234, R 733, Sac and Fox Agency, National Archives.

23. Francis Tymany to Charles E. Mix, May 6, 1858, RG 75, M 234, R 733, Sac and Fox Agency, National Archives; Committee on Indian Affairs, House Resolution No. 865, 33rd Cong., 2nd Sess., RG 46, Records of the United States Senate, National Archives.

24. Unratified Ottawa Treaty of 1857, manuscript copy, Department of Special Collections, Wichita State University Library.

25. *Baptist Missionary Magazine* 37, no. 7 (July, 1858): 271.

26. Kom-Chaw, John T. Jones, William Hurr, and Joseph King to A. M. Robinson, November 8, 1859; Perry Fuller to Robinson, November 10, 1859; Fuller to Robinson, February 23, 1860; Clinton C. Hutchinson to William P. Dole, August 13, 1862, RG 75, M 234, R 734-35, Sac and Fox Agency, National Archives.

27. Fuller to A. B. Greenwood, December 12, 1859, May 16, 1860, RG 75, M 234, R 734-35, Sac and Fox Agency, National Archives.

Chapter 5. The Grand Design

1. M. M. Marberry, *The Golden Voice: A Biography of Isaac Kalloch*, pp. 165-66; Andreas, *Kansas*, p. 258.

2. Jones to Dole, April 26, 1861; Hutchinson to Dole, April 30, 1861; Hutchinson to Branch, July 10 and September 20, 1861; undated (1861?) "Receipt"; three Sac and Fox chiefs (their marks) to Dole, September 10, 1861; John P. Usher to Dole, October 16, 1861, and Branch to Dole, November 20, 1862, RG 75, M 234, R 734, Sac and Fox Agency, National Archives.

3. Marberry, *The Golden Voice*, pp. 51-53, 110-20.

4. Ibid., pp. 145-49, 156-58, and 163ff. Haworth, whose *Ottawa University* has all the trappings of an in-house product, suggests that Marberry's biography of Kalloch was "given entirely to the muckracking style," Haworth, *Ottawa University*, nn. 20, 21. This indictment ignores Marberry's impressive list of contemporary newspapers, periodicals, pamphlets, and documents, which Haworth apparently considered unimportant. See Marberry, *The Golden Voice*, pp. 352-62; Hutchinson to Pratt, February 5, 1864, John G. Pratt Papers, Manuscript Division, Kansas State Historical Society, Topeka (microfilm edition, R 1).

5. Perry Fuller to A. B. Greenwood, August 11, 1860, and Kalloch, Jones, and William Hurr to Greenwood, n.d. (received January 14, 1861), RG 75, M 234, R 734, Sac and Fox Agency, National Archives; testimony of J. S. Emory before Enoch Hoag, December 1, 1869, RG 75, M 856, R 30, Target 2, Records Relating to an Investigation of Ottawa University, Records of the Central Superintendency of Indian Affairs, National Archives; Samuel LePage, *A Short History of Ottawa University*, pp. 4-6; W. R. Ir-

win, L. R. Smith, and J. A. Williamson to F. A. Walker, August 23, 1872, 42nd Cong., 3rd Sess., H. Doc. 31, *House Executive Documents*, vol. 3 (Serial 1565), p. 12; statement of William Hurr, February 2, 1882, RG 75, Special Case 95, National Archives.

6. Hutchinson to Dole, May 12, 1862, John P. Usher to Dole, October 16, 1862, RG 75, M 234, R 735, Sac and Fox Agency, National Archives; Hutchinson to Commissioner to Indian Affairs, December 24, 1863, RG 75, M 234, R 656, Ottawa Agency, National Archives; Kappler, *Indian Affairs*, 2:830-34.

7. Kappler, *Indian Affairs*, 2:831-32; Hutchinson to Commissioner of Indian Affairs, December 24, 1863, RG 75, M 234, R 656, Ottawa Agency, National Archives.

8. Kappler, *Indian Affairs*, 2:831-32.

9. Marberry, *The Golden Voice*, p. 167; W. R. Irwin, L. R. Smith, and J. A. Williamson to F. A. Walker, August 23, 1872, 42nd Cong., 3rd Sess., H. Doc. 31, *Executive Document*, 3:12.

10. John P. Usher to William Dole, September 10 and October 16, 1862; three Sac and Fox chiefs to Dole, September 10, 1862; Hutchinson to Dole, January 10, 1863, January 20, 1864, RG 75, M 234, R 735, Sac and Fox Agency, National Archives; Hutchinson to Dole, March 21, 1863, November 1, 1864, RG 75, M 234, R 656, National Archives; Usher to Dole, October 16, 1862, RG 48, M 606, R 4, Letters Sent by the Indian Division, Interior Department, National Archives; Usher to Dole, November 3, 1862, marked "*private*," RG 48, Box 11, Letters Received by the Indian Division, Interior Department, National Archives.

11. Jones, Wind, Hurr, Henry Clay, David Barnett, Wolfe, and fifteen additional Ottawa leaders to Dole, January 26, 1863, RG 75, M 234, R 734, Sac and Fox Agency, National Archives; Jones to Dole, May 21, 1863, Hutchinson to Dole, June 11, 13, 18, August 21, and December 5, 1863; Hutchinson to Charles E. Mix, October 5, 1863; Wind, Hurr, and Jones to Dole, January 26, 1864, RG 75, M 234, R 656, Ottawa Agency, National Archives.

12. Antoine Gorkey (accompanied by John Wilson's mark) to Secretary of the Interior, January 30, 1864, and Hutchinson to Dole, June 23, 1864, RG 75, M 234, R 656, Ottawa Agency, National Archives; meetings of September 9 and 16, 1864, Ottawa Town Company Minutes, Manuscript Division, Kansas State Historical Society; meetings of September 12, 1864, February 7, May 20, 24, and 26, 1865, minutes of the Ottawa University Board of Trustees, Business Office Vault, Ottawa University, Ottawa, Kansas.

13. Hutchinson to Dole, January 30, 1864, Jones to Usher, March

21, 1864, RG 75, M 234, R 656, Ottawa Agency, National Archives.

14. J. F. Goodin (certified by John Wilson's mark and those of several other Ottawa leaders) to Usher, August 22, 1864, Goodin (for the "majority" of Ottawas) to Usher, September 29, 1864, RG 75, M 234, R 656, Ottawa Agency, National Archives.

15. Wind, Clay, Hurr, and Wolfe to Dole, June 23, 1864; Gorkey, Goodin and twenty-seven Ottawas to Commissioner of Indian Affairs, July 19, 1863; William Albin's "Report" to Commissioner of Indian Affairs, January 5, 1865, all in RG 75, M 234, R 656, Ottawa Agency, National Archives; Hutchinson to Albin, [February ?,] 1865, RG 75, M 234, R 794, Schools, 1865, National Archives.

16. Hutchinson to Dennis N. Cooley, August 4, 1865; Hutchinson to Commissioner of Indian Affairs, September 20, 1865; Hutchinson to Thomas Murphy, December 3, 1866; Murphy to Lewis V. Bogy, December 7, 1866, RG 75, M 234, R 656-57, Ottawa Agency, National Archives.

17. *Western Home Journal* (Ottawa, Kansas), January 18, April 5, May 17, and August 23, 1866.

Chapter 6. The Perils of Providence

1. W. R. Irwin to O. H. Browning, March 6, 1867, RG 75, M 234, R 657, Ottawa Agency, National Archives; Charles Mix to Browning, August 15, 1867, RG 48, Letters Received by the Indian Division, Box 19, National Archives; I. S. Kalloch to Browning, February 13, 1867, RG 48, M 825, R 23, Selected Classes of Letters Received by the Indian Division, Interior Department, National Archives.

2. Kalloch to Lewis Bogy, March 21, 1867, RG 75, M 234, R 657, Ottawa Agency, National Archives; Irwin to Browning, May 7, 1867, Asa Lathrop to Browning, May 7, 1867, RG 75, Special Case 126, Ottawa University, National Archives; Ottawa University Board of Trustees Minutes, May 7, 1867, University Business Office Vault, Ottawa University.

3. Kalloch to Browning, April 20, 1867, RG 75, Special Case 126, National Archives; Ottawa University Minutes, April 22 and May 7, 1867; Bowles and Mason to W. R. Irwin, May 23, 1867, Bowles and Mason to Browning, May 24, 1867, Hutchinson to Secretary of the Interior, May 20, 1867, RG 75, M 234, R 657, Ottawa Agency, National Archives.

4. Kappler, *Indian Affairs*, 2:960-67.

5. Ibid.

6. Kalloch to C. E. Mix, November 22, 1867, Kalloch to Browning, April 20, 1867, RG 75, Special Case 126, National Archives.

7. Secretary of the Interior to N. G. Taylor, July 30, 1867, RG 75, M 234, R 657, Ottawa Agency, National Archives; *Western Home Journal*, July 25, 1867, April 30, June 18, and June 25, 1868; Ottawa University Minutes, February 17, 1868.

8. Ottawa University Minutes, January 28, 1868.

9. *Portrait and Biographical Record of Leavenworth, Douglas and Franklin Counties, Kansas*, 377.

10. Ottawa University Minutes, February 17, 1868.

11. Atkinson to N. G. Taylor, February 6, 1869, RG 75, Special Case 126, National Archives; Ottawa University Minutes, January 13, 1869.

12. Rev. Gillette to O. H. Browning, January 6, 1869, RG 48, M 825, R 23, Selected Classes of Letters Received by the Indian Division, Interior Department, National Archives.

13. John Wilson, James Wind, and Joseph King to Albert Wiley, January 20, 1869; Wilson, Wind, and William Hurr to Taylor, February 3, 1869; Atkinson to Browning, February 10, 1869; Ottawa delegation to Taylor, February 12, 1869; Atkinson to Secretary of Interior, April 13, 1869; Board of Trustees to Secretary of Interior, March 13 and April 21, 1869; A. N. Blacklidge to J. D. Cox, March 17, 1869, RG 75, Special Case 126, National Archives.

14. Board of Trustees to Secretary of Interior, March 13, 1869, RG 75, Special Case 126, National Archives.

15. C. N. Blacklidge to J. D. Cox, March 17, 1869, Atkinson to Taylor, March 1, 1869, S. S. Beroker to S. S. Warner, March 9, 1869, RG 75, Special Case 126, National Archives.

16. Ottawa University Minutes, April 1, May 22, 1869; *Argument of A. N. Blacklidge, in Behalf of the Ottawa Indians of Blanchard's Fork and Roche de Boeuf, in the Matter of the Ottawa University, or Indian School, at Ottawa, Kansas*, Department of Special Collections, Wichita State University Library; Petition of Citizens of Ottawa, January, 1869, and Board of Trustees to Secretary of Interior, April 21, 1869, RG 75, Special Case 126, National Archives; Minutes of the Euphemian Society, April 22, December 30, 1870, Business Office Vault, Ottawa University, Ottawa, Kansas.

17. Atkinson to Cox, July 22, 1869, RG 75, Special Case 126, National Archives; statement of S. A. Riggs, May 12, 1869, and Wilson, Wind, Hurr, et. al. to Commissioner of Indian Affairs, May

19, 1869, RG 75, M 234, R 657, Ottawa Agency, National Archives; Ottawa University Minutes, October 18, 1872. The record in the minutes of Jones's death demonstrates the obvious misunderstanding of later historians of the university. In the minute book is written in the margin "Jones died in 1873," evidently an attempt by someone later to correct the original minutes. Other evidence (notably W. R. Irwin's report of August 23, 1872, in RG 75, Special Case 126, National Archives) makes it clear that Jones died on August 16, 1872, and that the October 18, 1872, meeting was held to find a replacement on the board.

18. Jones to U. S. Grant, April 29, 1869, RG 75, M 234, R 647, Ottawa Agency, National Archives; statement of Jones, May 20, 1869, Jones to E. S. Parker, July 15, 1869, Atkinson to J. D. Cox, July 22, 1869, RG 75, Special Case 126, National Archives.

Chapter 7. Machinations Magnified

1. Nathan Bishop to J. D. Cox, July 29, 1869, RG 75, Special Case 126, National Archives.

2. Hutchinson to Cox, September 20, 1869, RG 75, Special Case 126, National Archives; W. T. Otto to E. C. Banfield, May 11, 1869; motion of Albert Horton, May 25, 1869, *U.S. v. C. C. Hutchinson, Late Indian Agent,* all in RG 206, Suit File, Records of the Solicitor of the Treasury, 1869-1884, National Archives. There are more docket books and other, mainly procedural, documents in the Federal Records Center, Kansas City.

3. Hutchinson to Cox, October 1, 1869, RG 75, Special Case 126, National Archives.

4. Enoch Hoag to E. S. Parker, January 13, 1870, RG 75, M 856, R 30, Central Superintendency Files, 1869-70, National Archives.

5. Ibid.

6. Ibid.

7. J. A. Williamson to Secretary of the Interior, October 13, 1869, Hutchinson to E. S. Parker, January 31, 1870, A. N. Blacklidge to Parker, February 3, 1870, transcript of Hoag hearing, January 6, 1870, F. S. Emory to Cox, May 4, 1870, Hoag to Cox, May 5, 1870, Hutchinson to Cox, March 10, 1870, all in RG 75, Special Case 126, National Archives; twenty Indians to Hoag, November 3, 1869, and Cox to Hoag, June 8, 1870, RG 75, Special Case 95, National Archives; ad circular [January 1870] and Joseph

Pooler et. al. to Commissioner of Indian Affairs, February 11, 1869, RG 75, M 234, R 657-58, Ottawa Agency, National Archives.

8. *Ottawa* (Kans.) *Journal,* April 21, 1870.

9. Hoag to Parker, January 13, 1870, RG 206, Suit File, Records of the Solicitor of the Treasury, 1869-84, National Archives; depositions of William Hurr, September 8, 1879, Henry Clay, September 18, 1879, John Earley, September 17, 1879, Andrew Glover, September 26, 1879, James Clark, September 9, 1879, Francis King, September 18, 1879, RG 75, Special Case 126, National Archives.

10. J. T. Jones to Jacob D. Cox, June 21, 1870, Atkinson to Cox, May 6, 1870, Hoag to Cox, June 23, 1870, W. T. Reynolds to Cox, May 30, 1870, Hoag to Parker, July 19, 1870, RG 75, Special Case 126, National Archives.

11. *Argument of Henry Beard, Esq., Before Jacob D. Cox, Secretary of the Interior. In the Matter of the Ottawa* [sic] *University, Kansas, its Location, and Endowment—Its Board of Trustees Legally Organized and fully Recognized by the United States and the Indians,* RG 75, Special Case 126, National Archives.

12. *Argument of A. N. Blacklidge, In Behalf of the Ottawa Indians of Blanchard's Fork and Roche de Boeuf, in the Matter of the Ottawa University, or Indian School at Ottawa Kansas,* in Department of Special Collections, Wichita State University Library.

13. Henry Beard, *Reply of the Ottawa University . . . To the Petition of the Ottawa Indians,* RG 75, Special Case 126, National Archives.

14. "D. N. C." [D. N. Cooley] to James Harlan, April 23, 1866, RG 75, Special Case 126, National Archives; Wilson et. al. to Commissioner of Indian Affairs, April 2, 1866, Hutchinson to Murphy, January 22, 1866, RG 75, M 234, R 657, Ottawa Agency, National Archives; Hutchinson to John Pratt, February 5, 1864, Pratt Papers (microfilm ed., R 1), Kansas State Historical Society; *Ottawa Journal,* November 10, 1870, April 25, 1872. In 1870 Hutchinson was preparing a book on the resources of Kansas to be printed by an eastern press and distributed on railroad trains generally.

15. Hutchinson affidavit, June 9, 1971, RG 75, Special Case 126, National Archives; *Ottawa Journal,* July 20 and August 28, 1871; *New York Times,* May 24 and July 7, 1871.

16. Cox to Albert Horton, September 27, 1869, Horton to E. C. Banfield, October 11, 1870, Hutchinson to Banfield, December 19, 1871, Horton to Banfield (with ten enclosures), January 10, 1872, C. Delano to George Boutwell, January 26, 1872, stipulation of

Horton and Hutchinson, February 9, 1872, RG 75, Suit File, Records of the Solicitor of the Treasury, 1869-84, National Archives.
17. Daniel Wilder, *Annals of Kansas, 1541-1885*, passim under Albert H. Horton; Horton to Solicitor of the Treasury, April 3, 1884, Horton to Benjamin Brewster, March 20, 1884, RG 206, Suit File, Records of the Solicitor of the Treasury, 1869-84, National Archives.
18. J. Q. Smith to Secretary of the Interior, February 26, 1876, RG 75, Special Case 95, National Archives.

Chapter 8. Victory and Defeat

1. William Nicholson to Hoag, January 1, 1872, RG 75, Special Case 126, National Archives; *Senate Miscellaneous No. 5*, 42nd Cong., 1st Sess., 1872 (Serial 1467); Henry Beard, *Argument*, RG 75, Special Case 95, National Archives.
2. W. A. Buckingham to Delano, July 1, 1872, Atkinson to J. M. S. Williams, June 19, 1872, Edward Toby to Delano, June 29, 1872, Roscoe Conkling to Delano (telegram), June 29, 1872, ? Backus to Delano, June 17, 1872, RG 75, Special Case 95, National Archives.
3. *Ottawa Journal*, July 4, 1872; *Lawrence* (Kans.) *Tribune*, July 6, 1872.
4. E. C. Taylor et. al. to President, July 31, 1872, T. C. Sears to Delano, August 1, 1872, RG 75, Special Case 95, National Archives; *Portrait and Biographical Record*, p. 377.
5. *Lawrence Tribune*, June 30, 1872; James A. Garfield, *The Diary of James A. Garfield*, ed. Harry Brown and Frederick Williams 2:66; J. P. C. Shanks to Secretary of Interior, telegram, August 2, 1872, RG 75, Special Case 95, National Archives.
6. W. R. Irwin to F. A. Walker, August 5, 1872, Hoag to Irwin, August 15, 1872, report by Irwin, L. R. Smith, and W. A. Williamson, August 23, 1872, RG 75, Special Case 126, National Archives; statement of Atkinson, August 19, 1872, RG 75, Special Case 95, National Archives.
7. Francis King et. al. to Commissioner of Indian Affairs, October 5, 1872, RG 75, M 234, R 658, Ottawa Agency, National Archives; Delano to James Harlan, December 7, 1872, George Williams to Delano, November 27, 1872, RG 75, Special Case 126, National Archives; *Portrait and Biographical Record*, p. 377.
8. Ottawa University Minutes, December 28, 1872; *Proceedings of the National Baptist Convention, Held in the First Baptist Church*

of Philadelphia, May 28, 29, and 30th, 1872, pp. 183-84.

9. William Hayes to Irwin, July 17, 1873, RG 75, Special Case 126, National Archives.

10. S. S. Cutting to Delano, March 22, 1873, RG 75, Special Case 95, National Archives; Francis King to Irwin, June 28, 1873, Thacher and Stevens to E. Washburn, August 26, 1873, RG 75, Special Case 126, National Archives; Ottawa University Minutes, July 30, 1873.

11. Enoch Hoag to Delano, October 23 and 29, 1873, and copies of agreement of October 29, 1873, RG 75, Special Case 95, National Archives.

12. Board of American Baptist Home Mission Society to Secretary of the Interior, July 28, 1874, S. S. Cutting to Z. Chandler, December 21, 1876, RG 75, Special Case 95, National Archives; Ottawa University Minutes, May 26 and June 23, 1874.

13. William Clark to P. B. Plumb, April 9, 1878, RG 75, Special Case 95, National Archives.

14. Hoag to Delano, July 23, 1878, RG 75, Special Case 126, National Archives; Ottawa Attorneys to U.S. District Court (Kansas), Case File No. 543, "Ottawa Indian Lands," Federal Records Center, Kansas City.

15. John Earley to C. G. Foster, February 3, 1883, order of Foster, March 4, 1883, Case File No. 543, "Ottawa Indian Lands," Federal Records Center, Kansas City; J. W. McGowan to Commissioner of General Land Office, March 15, 1902, RG 75, Special Case 95, National Archives.

16. *Ottawa* (Kans.) *Republican,* February 12, 1874.

Chapter 9. Legal Atonement

1. Kappler, *Indian Affairs,* 2:830-31.

2. Ibid., p. 964.

3. Joseph B. King, "The Ottawa Indians in Kansas and Oklahoma," *Collections of the Kansas State Historical Society,* 13:377; H. Craig Miner, *The St. Louis–San Francisco Transcontinental Railroad: The Thirty-Fifth Parallel Project, 1853-1890,* pp. 79-80.

4. 23 Stat. 388-391 (1887), 26 Stat. 794-96 (1891), 26 Stat. 1010 (1891), *Congressional Record* 23, pt. 1; 957, and 23, pt. 2; 1665, 1704, 2015; executive order of February 17, 1927, Kappler, *Indian Affairs,* 4:1043.

5. Lawrence C. Kelly, "Cato Sells," in Kvasnicka and Viola,

eds., *Commissioners of Indian Affairs*, pp. 248-49; Cash and Wolff, *Ottawa People*, pp. 47-48, 56-63.

6. Washburn, *Red Man's Land*, pp. 102-104.

7. See, for example, the conflicting designations in the treaties of 1795, 1807, 1817, 1818, 1820, 1821, and 1833 in Kappler, *Indian Affairs*, 2:39, 92, 145, 162, 188, 198, and 410.

8. "Defendant's Request for Findings of Fact," Doc. 133, Indian Claims Commission, 20-21; "Opinion of the Commission," *Robert Dominic, et. al. v. United States*, and *The Ottawa Tribe and Guy Jennison, et. al. v. United States*, Consolidated Docs. 40-B, C, D, E, and F and 133, 2 Ind. Cl. Cm., p. 472, Library Division, Kansas State Historical Society; Feest and Feest, "Ottawa," in Bruce G. Trigger, ed., *Northeast*, vol. 15 of William G. Sturtevant, ed., *Handbook of North American Indians*.

9. "Opinion of the Commission," August 6, 1953, 2 Ind. Cl. Cm., pp., 473-80, Library Division, Kansas State Historical Society.

10. "Findings of Fact," August 6, 1953, 2 Ind. Cl. Cm., pp. 466-67.

11. Petition, "Trust Lands in Kansas, Doc. 303, Indian Claims Commission, pp. 2-3, Library Division, Kansas State Historical Society.

12. Ibid., pp. 1-13; Imre Sutton, *Indian Land Tenure: Bibliographical Essays and Guide to the Literature*, p. 93.

13. Theodore W. Taylor, *The States and Their Indian Citizens*, pp. 50-62; S. Lyman Tyler, *A History of Indian Policy*, pp. 148-72; Patricia K. Ourada, "Dillion Seymour Myer," in Kvasnicka and Viola, eds., *Commissioners of Indian Affairs*, pp. 293-95; House Concurrent Resolution 108, *Congressional Record*, 83rd Cong., 1st Sess., 99 (August 1, 1953): 9968, 10815.

14. Tyler, *A History of Indian Policy*, pp. 172-73; Washburn, *Red Man's Land*, pp. 89-99; Cash and Wolff, *Ottawa People*, pp. 68-71; *Federal Register*, August 13, 1959, pp. 6587-6593.

15. Patricia K. Ourada, "Glen L. Emmons," in Kvasnicka and Viola, eds., *Commissioners of Indian Affairs*, pp. 304-305; Cash and Wolff, *Ottawa People*, pp. 69-71; 70 Stat. 943 (1956); *Federal Register*, August 13, 1959; *Investigation of the Bureau of Indian Affairs*, 82nd Cong., 2nd Sess., H. Rept. 2503, Union Calendar no. 790, p. 893. For another example of an attempt to use ICC claims to force Indian people to vote in favor of termination, see Robert C. Carriker, "The Kalispel Tribe and the Indian Claims Commission Experience," *Western Historical Quarterly* 9, no. 1 (January, 1978): 19-31.

16. "Petitioner's Proposed Findings of Fact," Doc. 303, ICC, pp. 56-57, Native American Rights Fund, Boulder, Colo.

17. Ibid., pp. 8, 56-57. For an analysis of the "fair and honest dealings" section of the Indian CI Act, see J. M. Kelly, "Indians —the Extent of the 'Fair and Honest Dealings Section' of the Indian Claims Commission Act," *Saint Louis University Law Journal,* vol. 15, no. 3 (1971), 491-507.

18. "Opinion," Doc. 303, 8 Ind. Cl. Cm. 830-31; "Interloctory Order," ibid., 899-a-899-b.

19. "On Defendant's Motion for Rehearing," Doc. 303, 9 Ind. Cl. Cm. 98-107.

20. "Amended Final Award," Doc. 303, 14 Ind. Cl. Cm. 677-78; 81 Stat. 166 (1967).

21. Driver, *Ottawa University Bulletin,* 77-78.

Bibliography

Manuscript Materials

Washington, D.C. National Archives
RG 46.   M 386. Records of the United States Senate.
RG 48.   Letters Received by the Indian Division, Interior
           Department, 1862-1867, boxes 11, 19.
           M 825. Selected Classes of Letters Received by
           the Indian Division, Interior Department, 1867,
           R 23.
           M 606. Letters Sent by the Indian Division, In-
           terior Department, 1862, R 4.
RG 75.   M 856. Target 2. Central Superintendency Files,
           1869-1870 (R 30).
           M234. Letters Received by the Office of Indian
           Affairs, Ottawa Agency, 1863-1869 (R 656-58).
           Letters Received by the Office of Indian Affairs,
           Sac and Fox Agency, 1854-1864, R 733-735.
           Schools, 1865, R 794.
           Special Case Files: Special Case 95: Correspon-
           dence, 1872-1902. Special Case 126: *Argu-
           ment of Henry Beard, Esq., Before Hon. Jacob
           D. Cox, Secretary of the Interior. In the Matter
           of the Ottowa* [sic] *University, Kansas, Its Lo-
           cation, and Endowment — Its Board of Trustees*

Legally Organized and fully Recognized by the United States and the Indians. Washington, D.C.: Judd & Detweiler, Printers, 1870. Henry Beard, "Reply of the Ottawa University . . . To the Petition of the Ottawa Indians." N.p., n.d. Correspondence, 1867-1870.

    Target 949. Documents Relating to the Negotiations of Unratified Treaties, 1821-1865, R 8.

RG 206   Suit File, Records of the Solicitor of the Treasury, 1869-1884.

Topeka, Kansas, Kansas State Historical Society.
  Manuscript Division
    Isaac McCoy Papers (microfilm ed., R 1-9).
    Jotham Meeker Papers (microfilm ed., R 1-2).
    John G. Pratt Papers (microfilm ed., R 1).
    Ottawa Town Company Minutes
  Library Division:
    "Trust Lands in Kansas." Petition, Docket 303, Indian Claims Commission, *The Ottawa Tribe and Guy Jennison, et. al., v., United States,* August 10, 1951.

Wichita, Kans., Wichita State University Library, Department of Special Collections. Manuscript copy of unratified Ottawa Treaty of 1857.

Kansas City, Missouri, Federal Records Center. "Ottawa Indian Lands." Case File No. 543.

Ottawa, Kansas, Ottawa University. University Business Office Vault. Minutes of the Ottawa University Board of Trustees. Minutes of the Euphemian Society.

Middle Amana, Iowa, Amana Historical Society. Christian Metz Diary.

Published Government Documents

American State Papers. Class II. Indian Affairs. Vols. 1, 2. Washington, D.C. Gales and Seaton, 1832 and 1834.
Congressional Record.
House Executive Document No. 31, 42nd Cong., 3rd Sess., Vol. 3

(Serial 1565).

Henry Beard. *Argument of Henry Beard, Esq., Before Hon. Jacob D. Cox, Secretary of the Interior. In the Matter of the Ottowa [sic] University, Kansas, Its Location, and Endowment—Its Board of Trustees Legally Organized and fully Recognized by the United States and the Indians.* Washington, D.C.: Judd & Detweiler, Printers, 1870.

A. N. Blacklidge. *Argument of A. N. Blacklidge, in Behalf of the Ottawa Indians of Blanchard's Fork and Roche de Boeuf, in the Matter of the Ottawa University, or Indian School at Ottawa, Kansas.* Washington, D.C.: Cunningham & McIntosh, 1870.

Congressional Record

House Executive Document No. 31, 42nd Cong., 3rd Sess., Vol. 3 (Serial 565).

Indian Claims Commission Decisions. Vols. 2, 8, 14, 30. Boulder, Colo.: Native American Rights Fund, n.d.

Investigation of the Bureau of Indian Affairs, 82nd Cong., 2nd Sess., House Report No. 2503, Union Calendar No. 790, Washington, D.C.: Government Printing Office, 1953.

Journals of the Continental Congress, 1774-1789. Edited by Gailland Hunt. Washington, D.C.: Government Printing Office, 1902-1937.

Senate Miscellaneous No. 5, 42nd Cong., 1st Sess. (Serial 1467).

Special Subcommittee on Indian Education, Committee on Labor and Public Welfare, *Indian Education: A National Tragedy—A National Challenge,* 91st Cong., 1st Sess., Senate Report no. 501.

U.S. Stat. at Large.

Newspapers and Contemporary Magazines

Baptist Missionary Magazine (Boston, Mass.), 1838-58.
Lawrence (Kans.) *Tribune* (Lawrence, Kans.), 1871-73.
New York (N.Y.) *Times, 1869-72.*
Ottawa (Kans.) *Journal,* 1870-72.

Ottawa (Kans.) *Republican,* 1874.

Western Home Journal (Ottawa, Kans.), 1865-69.

Books and Theses

Andreas, A. T. *The History of the State of Kansas.* Chicago: A. T. Andreas, 1883.

Barry, Louise, comp. *The Beginning of the West: Annals of the Kansas Gateway to the American West, 1540-1854.* Topeka: Kansas State Historical Society, 1972.

Beckman, Peter. *Kansas Monks: A History of St. Benedict's Abbey.* Atchison, Kans.: Abbey Student Press, 1957.

Berkhofer, Robert F., Jr. *Salvation and the Savage: An Analysis of Protestant Missions and American Indian Response, 1787-1862.* Lexington: University of Kentucky Press, 1965.

Boorstin, Daniel J. *The Americans: The National Experience.* New York: Random House, 1965.

Bourne, Edward G., ed., and Annie N. Bourne, trans. *The Voyages and Explorations of Samuel de Champlain, 1604-1616.* Vol. 1. New York: Allerton Book Co., 1922.

Cash, Joseph H., and Gerald W. Wolff. *The Ottawa People.* Phoenix, Ariz.: Indian Tribal Series, 1976.

Clifton, James A. *The Prairie People: Continuity and Change in Potawatomi Indian Culture, 1665-1965.* Lawrence: Regents Press of Kansas, 1977.

Correspondence on the Subject of the Emigration of Indians, Between the 30th November, 1831, and 27 December, 1833, with Abstracts of by Disbursing Agents in the Removal and Subsistence of Indians, etc., etc. Vol. 2. Washington, D.C.: Duff Green, 1825.

Downes, Randolph C. *Council Fires on the Upper Ohio.* Pittsburgh, Pa.: University of Pittsburgh Press, 1940.

Driver, Russ, ed. *1976-1977 Catalog Issue. Ottawa University Bulletin* 73, no. 1: 1976.

Edmunds, R. David. *The Potawatomis: Keepers of the Fire.* Norman: University of Oklahoma Press, 1978.

Foreman, Grant. *The Last Trek of the Indians.* Chicago: University of Chicago Press, 1946.

Garfield, James A. *The Diary of James A. Garfield,* ed. Harry Brown and Frederick Williams. Vol. 2. Lansing: University of Michigan Press, 1967.

Gates, Paul Wallace. *Fifty Million Acres: Conflicts over Kansas Land Policy, 1854-1890.* Ithaca, N.Y.: Cornell University Press, 1954.

Haworth, B. Smith. *Ottawa University: Its History and Its Spirit.* Ottawa, Kans.: Ottawa University, 1957.

Hill, Edward E. *The Office of Indian Affairs, 1824-1880: Historical Sketches.* New York: Clearwater Publishing Company, Inc., 1974.

Horsman, Reginald. *Expansion and American Indian Policy, 1774-1789.* East Lansing: Michigan State University Press, 1967.

Jacobs, Wilbur R. *Dispossessing the American Indian: Indians and Whites on the Colonial Frontier.* New York: Charles Scribner's Sons, 1972.

Jennings, Francis. *The Invasion of America: Indians, Colonialism, and the Cant of Conquest.* Chapel Hill: University of North Carolina Press, 1975.

Kappler, Charles, comp. *Indian Affairs, Laws and Treaties.* Vols. 2, 4. Washington, D.C.: Government Printing Office, 1904.

Kennedy, Gail, ed. *Education for Democracy: The Debate over the Report of the President's Commission on Higher Education.* Boston: D. C. Heath, 1952.

Kvasnicka, Robert M., and Herman J. Viola. *The Commissioners of Indian Affairs, 1824-1977.* Lincoln: University of Nebraska Press, 1979.

LePage, Samuel M. *A Short History of Ottawa University.* N.p., 1929.

McCoy, Isaac. *History of Baptist Missions: Embracing Remarks on the Former and Present Conditions of the Aboriginal Tribes: Their Former Settlement Within the Indian Territory, and Their Future Prospects.* Washington, D.C.: William M. Morrison, 1840.

McGee, John W. *The Catholic Church in the Grand River Valley, 1833-1950.* Lansing, Mich.: Franklin DeKlein Co., 1950.

McMurtrie, Douglas C., and Albert H. Allen. *Jotham Meeker, Pioneer Printer of Kansas.* Chicago: Eyncourt Press, 1930.

Marberry, M. M. *The Golden Voice: A Biography of Isaac Kalloch.* New York: Farrar, Straus and Co., 1947.

Miner, H. Craig. *The St. Louis-San Francisco Transcontinental Railroad: The Thirty-fifth Parallel Project, 1853-1890.* Lawrence, Manhattan, and Wichita: University Press of Kansas, 1972.

———. and William E. Unrau. *The End of Indian Kansas: A Study of Cultural Revolution, 1854-1871.* Lawrence: Regents Press of Kansas, 1978.

Morgan, Lewis Henry. *The Indian Journals, 1859-62.* Edited by Leslie A. White. Ann Arbor: University of Michigan Press, 1959.

Morse, Jedidiah. *Report to the Secretary of War of the United States, on Indian Affairs, Comprising a Narrative of a Tour Performed in the Summer of 1820, under a Commission for the President of the United States for the Purpose of Ascertaining for the Use of the Government, the Actual State of the Indian Tribes in Our Country.* New Haven, Conn.: S. Converse, 1822.

The Oxford English Dictionary. Vols. 4, 11. London: Oxford at the Clarendon Press, 1961.

Peckham, Howard H. *Pontiac and the Indian Uprising.* Princeton, N.J.: Princeton University Press, 1947.

Phillips, Paul Chrisler. *The Fur Trade.* Vol. I. Norman: University of Oklahoma Press, 1961.

Portrait and Biographical Record of Leavenworth, Douglas, and Franklin Counties, Kansas. Chicago: Chapman Publishing Co., 1899.

Proceedings of the National Baptist Convention, Held in the First Baptist Church of Philadelphia, May 28, 29, and 30th, 1872. New York: Sheldon & Co., 1872.

Prucha, Francis P. *American Indian Policy in the Formative Years: The Indian Trade and Intercourse Acts, 1790-1834.* Cambridge, Mass.: Harvard University Press, 1962.

Richardson, James D., comp. *A Compilation of the Messages and Papers of the Presidents.* Vols. 1, 3. New York: Bureau of National Literature, 1897.

Rohrbough, Malcolm J. *The Land Office Business: The Settlement and Administration of American Public Lands, 1789-1837.* New York: Oxford University Press, 1968.

Royce, Charles C., comp. *Indian Land Cessions in the United States.* Washington, D.C.: Government Printing Office, 1899.

Schoolcraft, Henry R. *Historical Sketches and Statistical Information Respecting the History, Conditions and Prospects of the Indian Tribes of the United States.* Pt. 1. Philadelphia: Lippincott, Grambo & Co., 1851.

———. *Personal Memoirs of a Residence of Thirty Years with the Indian Tribes on the American Frontiers: With Brief Notices of Passing Events, Facts, and Opinions, A.D. 1812 to 1842.* Philadelphia: Lippincott, Grambo, and Co., 1851.

Schultz, George A. *An Indian Canaan: Isaac McCoy and the Vision of an Indian State.* Norman: University of Oklahoma Press, 1972.

Sheehan, Bernard W. *Seeds of Extinction: Jeffersonian Philanthropy and the American Indian.* Chapel Hill: University of North Carolina Press, 1973. Reprint. W. W. Norton & Company, Inc., 1974.

Smith, B. Haworth. *Ottawa University: Its History and Its Spirit.* Ottawa, Kans.: Ottawa University, 1957.

Starburg, Robert E. "Baptists on the Kansas Frontier." B.D. thesis, Northern Baptist Theological Seminary, 1960. Typed copy, Library Division, Kansas State Historical Society.

Stearn, E. Wagner, and Allen E. Stearn. *The Effect of Smallpox on the Destiny of the Amerindian.* Boston: Bruce Humphries, Inc., 1945.

Sutton, Imre. *Indian Land Tenure: Bibliographical Essays and Guide to the Literature.* New York: Clearwater Publishing Company, 1975.

Taylor, Theodore W. *The States and Their Indian Citizens.* Washington, D.C.: Government Printing Office, 1972.

Tewksbury, Donald G. *The Founding of American Colleges and Universities before the Civil War.* New York: Teachers College, Columbia University, 1932. Reprint. New York: Archon Books, 1965.

Thwaites, Reuben Gold, ed. *The Jesuit Relations and Allied Documents, Travels, and Explorations of the Jesuit Missionaries in New France.* Vols. 39, 49, 50, 54, 55. New York: Pageant Book Co., 1959.

Trigger, Bruce G., ed. *Northeast,* Vol. 15 of William C. Sturtevant, ed., *Handbook of North American Indians.* Washington, D.C.: Smithsonian Institution, 1978.

Tyler, S. Lyman. *A History of Indian Policy.* Washington, D.C.: Government Printing Office, 1973.

Viola, Herman. *Thomas L. McKenney, Architect of America's Early Indian Policy, 1816-1830.* Chicago: Swallow Press, Inc., 1974.

Washburn, Wilcomb E. *Red Man's Land/White Man's Law.* New York: Charles Scribner's Sons, 1971.

Wilder, Daniel, comp. *Annals of Kansas, 1541-1885.* Topeka: Kansas State Historical Society, 1886.

Articles

Bauman, Robert F. "The Migration of the Ottawa Indians from the Maumee Valley to Walpole Island." *Northwest Ohio Quarterly* 21 (Spring, 1949): 86-112.

———. "Kansas, Canada, or Starvation." *Michigan History* 36 (September, 1952): 287-99.

———. "The Removal of Indians from the Maumee Valley: A Selection from the Dresden W. H. Howard Papers." *Northwest Ohio Quarterly* 30 (Winter, 1957-58): 10-25.

Bolt, Robert. "Reverend Leonard Slater in the Grand Valley." *Michigan History* 51 (Fall, 1967): 241-48.

Carriker, Robert C. "The Kalispel Tribe and the Indian Claims Commission Experience." *Western Historical Quarterly* 9 (January, 1978): 19-31.

Cook, Sherburne F. "The Significance of Disease in the Extinction of the New England Indians." *Human Biology* 45 (1973): 485-508.

Gates, Paul W. "Indian Allotments Preceding the Dawes Act," in John G. Clark, ed., *The Frontier Challenge: Responses to the Trans-Mississippi West*. Lawrence, Manhattan, and Wichita: University Press of Kansas, 1971.

Kelly, J. M. "Indians—The Extent of the 'Fair and Honest Dealings' Section of the Indian Claims Commission Act." *Saint Louis University Law Journal* 15 (1971): 491-507.

King, Joseph B. "The Ottawa Indians in Kansas and Oklahoma." *Collections of the Kansas State Historical Society* 13 (1913-14): 373-78.

Paré, George. "The St. Joseph Mission." *Mississippi Valley Historical Review* 17 (June, 1930): 24-54.

Prucha, Francis P. "Thomas McKenney and the New York Indian Board." *Mississippi Valley Historical Review* 48 (March, 1962): 635-55.

Rouse, Shelly D. "Colonel Dick Johnson's Choctaw Academy: A Forgotten Educational Experiment." *Ohio Archeological and Historical Society Publication* 35 (January, 1916): 88-117.

Index

Alcohol: 18, 27, 33-34, 44, 55, 60, 67, 161
Alderson, L. A.: 82-83
Allotments: 161-63
Allouez, Claude: 14, 43-44
American Baptist Home Mission Society: 39, 78, 80, 111-13, 142, 147, 153-54, 172; and final settlement, 155-56
American Board of Foreign Missions: 31, 39, 42, 49, 51, 58-62, 72
American Indian Mission Association: 59
Atkinson, Robert: 8, 141-43, 155, 172, 175; arrival at Ottawa, 112-13, 129, 138; defense of university to 1869, 114-24; later actions to hold university, 126, 131-33; and congressional investigation (1872), 147, 149-52
Auglaize River: 12, 21, 27, 30, 34
Augooshaway (Ottawa tribal leader): 24
Autokee (Ottawa chief): 57-58, 63-64

Baptist Board of Foreign Missions: see American Board of Foreign Missions
Baptist Church: 9, 81, 84, 117, 126, 130, 141, 163, 172, 176; and Indian education, 35, 39, 43, 45, 70-71; and Isaac McCoy, 45-62; and Jotham Meeker, 60-73; and Ottawa University founding, 75, 79, 82-83, 88-90; and Ottawa Board 1867-69, 111-24, 139; and late defense, 136; and congressional investigation, 147-54; see also American Board of Foreign Missions and American Baptist Home Mission Society
Baptist Home Mission Board: see American Baptist Home Mission Society
Baptist Home Mission Society: see American Baptist Home Mission Society
Beard, Henry: 152; briefs by, 136-42
Blacklidge, C. N.: 118, 122-23, 132; briefs by 136-42
Blanchard's Fork: 24, 53, 55, 168; see also Auglaize River
Bluemont Central College: 80

207